TRANSPORTATION

in Central New York and the Baldwinsville Area

⊶ 1600 to 1940 ⊷

By Robert W. Bitz

LCCN: 2012913843
ISBN-13: 978-0-9859504-0-8
First edition, published 2012.

Ward Bitz Publishing
Baldwinsville, New York

The author may be contacted at:
P.O. Box 302
Plainville, New York 13137

Preface

Webster's Dictionary defines transportation as an act, process or instance of transporting or being transported. This definition is sufficiently broad to permit hundreds or even thousands of books to be written about transportation with each one different than the others. The title of this book narrows the geographic area of transportation to Central New York and the Baldwinsville area, during the years 1600 to 1940. Even with this narrowing, separate books could cover smaller geographic areas, shorter time periods and many topics that are a part of transportation.

With this in mind, the reader needs to recognize that this book is a primer, providing only a superficial glimpse of the remarkable changes that occurred in a relatively short period. The period shown in the title, 1600 to 1940, is twice what is covered in any depth. The earlier years are mentioned only to show the contrast, before substantial contact of white men with Native Americans, with the significant changes occurring when white settlements came to Central New York. During the period from 1600 to 1776, white men introduced horses, crude roads and slightly improved waterways to the Native Americans but these improvements had only minor effects upon the Native Americans' transportation.

Baldwinsville, by itself, provides an excellent place to feature the changes in transportation. The Seneca River, with its rapids (rifts) flowing through the village, provided a natural location for a dam to furnish power, industry to flourish and a canal to allow the continuance of navigation on the river. The river's connection with the Erie Canal, an early railroad passing through the village, a later second railroad, a trolley line and the Barge Canal all were important elements in the development of transportation in Baldwinsville that never touched many other communities in Central New York.

It would be inappropriate, however, to completely ignore the improvements in transportation taking place outside of the Baldwinsville area, because without those improvements little would have happened in Baldwinsville. The turnpikes, canals and railroads crisscrossing New York State brought people, goods and industry to Baldwinsville, and served as the arteries to transport products from Baldwinsville to the outside world.

It is unfortunate that photography did not become common until the latter part of the 1800s. Wouldn't it be wonderful to have photographs of settlers cutting their way through the forests on their way to Central New York, of Dr. and Mrs. Baldwin coming up the Seneca River and viewing for the first time what later became Baldwinsville, of 20 ox teams dragging a huge tree across the Seneca to help form the dam, and of immigrants toiling with shovels removing earth to form the canals? Only our imagination can give us pictures of these and hundreds of other events occurring in the early years of the local evolution in transportation.

It is hoped that this book will be a catalyst to spur the readers to create some mental images of their own where photographs are unavailable. There are a few engravings included that came from the minds of others, and numerous photographs from the late 1800s and early 1900s that help show the changes that took place in transportation during this period of time. The author apologizes for the lack of quality in some of the pictures but to adapt an old saying, 'a picture is worth a thousand words', we might say in the case of some of the pictures, 'this picture is worth only 500 words'.

When writing a book, many decisions need to be made regarding what to include and what to exclude. The last chapter of this book extends beyond the realm of the book's title. The author felt it inappropriate to totally ignore some important aspects in the history of transportation that wrap around what had been written in the earlier chapters. He hopes that the words that are written and the pictures included in this book will enrich each reader's knowledge of the dramatic changes in transportation and encourage further exploration of specific areas that are of special interest.

Acknowledgements

History is but a window into the past. Take a brief moment to look out a window near you. Something special may catch your eye or perhaps several things. In any case, there is far more outside the window than you were able to observe. So it is with history. Pictures and books provide us with a window into the past but, like the glance out of our window, provide us only a small portion of what has occurred.

Without the books and pictures from the past, even though they are only a small portion of what transpired, our lives would lack much of the richness we enjoy today. Without a road map telling us where we have been, it is difficult to know exactly where we are and the best direction to take in the future.

Authors, historians, artists and photographers, over several thousand years, have made it possible for each of us to look through untold numbers of windows into the past. We usually take their work fore granted but owe them many thanks. Life would be void of most of our learning and many of its joys if we could not look back in time.

Whenever I sit at my computer to write a book, I become increasingly thankful for the words and pictures that others have previously recorded. It is similar to having a bank full of money at my disposal to draw upon whenever I wish. Deposits have been made by thousands of people and they are mine and yours to be used whenever we wish. In addition, when a withdrawal is made from this bank of history, the deposits are increased because of what is being added.

While I will always be thankful to the thousands, both before and after Herodotus, that have recorded history, it was largely local historians who made this book possible. In its Bibliography the reader can see the printed sources that were used to obtain the necessary information. However, much of what I have written has come, in the course of living, from others whose names I cannot usually recall.

Local historians of the 19th and 20th centuries have provided the greater part of the material in this book and I am indebted to them. Bob Nostrant, Tony and Eleanor Christopher, Pearl Palmer and Ruth Connell were all my friends. The other authors have indirectly become my friends through reading their work.

Baldwinsville is blessed with a wonderful library containing a large collection of local history. The Shacksboro Schoolhouse holds treasures of old photographs and artifacts. Both of these sources have provided a wealth of material for this book.

Sue Ellen McManus is a walking encyclopedia of local history and has been a valuable resource for both material and editing. Debbie Stack edited my manuscript and made valuable suggestions for its organization and clarity. I am indebted to the Town Clerks of both Lysander and Van Buren as well as Lysander Historian Bonnie Kisselstein for the opportunity to go through their record vaults to obtain information regarding our roads and bridges. These records provided facts recorded at the time the history was made. I also appreciate the photos and illustrations of the stagecoach and early train era that Dick Palmer made available on the internet. I will admit that I used the internet to obtain occasional information but attempted to use only reliable sources. With information from many sources, undoubtedly I have overlooked and not mentioned some person or some source, and for this I apologize.

After exploring deeply into the history of transportation I must give my heartfelt thanks to the thousands of men and women who gave much of their lives in the development of the transportation system I enjoy today. They cut the trees, dug the canals, laid the railroad tracks, built the roads, made the wagons, automobiles, airports and dozens of other transportation related efforts that I accept with little thought. Each of us builds our life on the shoulders of people that were here before us, as well as those living today. My thanks go to each and everyone!

About the Author

Robert Bitz has lived on the farm in the Town of Lysander, settled by his ancestors in 1835, since he was born. He spent eight years at the two-room country school in Plainville and then rode on a school bus to attend Baldwinsville Academy for four years.

After graduating from Cornell University he came back to the family farm and developed the farm into a large, widely known business that manufactured a variety of turkey products that were marketed throughout the United States. Working with his son Mark Bitz, he also developed a feed-mill, in the adjacent Town of Elbridge, that manufactured feed for their turkeys and for numerous herds of dairy cattle in Central New York. They also owned and operated a cooking plant for their turkey products in the nearby Town of Salina.

In addition to a half century of manufacturing and farming, Bob has always had a deep interest in history. He has served as President of the New York State Agricultural Society, President of the Friends of the Witter Museum and been a member of several other history related organizations. Bob has been a member of the Town of Lysander Planning and Town Boards, gaining an insider's view into government's role in transportation. He has traveled extensively through many parts of the world and observed transportation in varied states of development. For a number of years he had a museum on his farm called 'The Pioneer Experience'.

During Bob's retirement he has written three books relating to the history of agriculture. Recently he wrote, *A History of Manufacturing in Baldwinsville and the Towns of Lysander and Van Buren*, which complements the material in this book. Bob also completed a book entitled, *Tales of a Turkey Farmer*, in which he shares a few memories of the development of Plainville Turkey Farm. He enjoys participating in a creative writing class in Florida during his winters and undoubtedly, in the future, will be applying more words to paper as he shares his memories and thoughts.

Transportation in Central New York and the Baldwinsville Area – 1600 to 1940

Travel Through the Wilderness

For centuries the main highways of New York were its many waterways and almost invisible Native American trails through the forests. Arguably there was no other State possessing such a complete system of natural waterways as that of New York. Thousands of years before man arrived in North America, glaciers shaped the face of what is now New York, leaving hills, valleys, lakes, streams and rivers. These valleys, with their natural bodies of water, provided avenues for ready-made transportation. They were first used by Native Americans, then by fur traders and missionaries and later by white settlers.

Central New York, upon the arrival of explorers, fur traders and early settlers, was "nature," in her original beauty, barely touched by the hands of man. There were no highways, utility poles, smokestacks, houses or prominent signs. It was a vast forest occasionally interrupted by rivers, lakes and streams. Scattered about were small Native American villages or clearings where villages had previously existed. A sharp eye could occasionally denote a foot path through the forests.

The Hudson River provided a direct waterway from the Atlantic Ocean at its mouth, north to what is now Albany. The Mohawk River, Wood Creek, Oneida Lake and Oswego River and Lake Ontario opened New York from Albany to the West. The St. Lawrence River, the Richelieu River in Quebec, Lake Champlain, Lake George and the upper portion of the Hudson River provided a gateway to Albany and Western New York from the North. The St. Lawrence River, flowing along many miles of New York's northern border, provided a direct route to Lake Ontario while the Oswego and the Genesee Rivers flowing into Lake Ontario were gateways to Western and Central New York. The Finger Lakes,

A portrayal of Central New York as it looked when roads were first cut through the forests.

numerous rivers and scattered lakes provided additional natural highways for travel inside the boundaries of New York. Although of less importance, the Susquehanna, emptying into the Chesapeake Bay with headwaters at Otsego Lake in Cooperstown, and the Delaware River, emptying into Delaware Bay, provided routes to and from the South.

Long distance travel on many of these waterways required portages over land. In much of Upstate New York, changes in elevation of several hundred feet or more, to sea level on the Hudson River at Albany, involved numerous small waterfalls and rapids that could not be negotiated on water. Even so, there were long navigable stretches of water without a portage including much of the Hudson River, Lake Ontario, Lake Champlain and Oneida Lake. Because these navigable waters were not sufficient to take man to all corners of the State, travel over land was necessary for the majority of settlers. Many families, including some of the author's ancestors, came to Central New York on foot during the late winter with their material possessions on an ox pulled sled.

Since Native American footpaths were the first system of roads used in Central New York, it was natural that the first white men would find them a helpful guide through the forests. Some of the roads white men cut through the forests followed major Indian trails, especially the trails around large bodies of water or to rifts that provided a convenient river crossing. They became parts of our first notable roadways, including the Great Genesee Road, the Seneca Turnpike and the Cherry Valley Turnpike, and today are still some of our major highways.

The most common method of travel by both Native Americans and early settlers was by foot. Because of trees, rocks, streams and swamp land, travel with wheeled vehicles was almost impossible. When traveling on natural waterways, the natives used canoes covered with elm bark or dugouts hollowed from a tree, that were light enough to be carried over portages. White men were forced to use similar sized vessels because of the portages.

Some examples of the experiences of early settlers help provide insight into the difficulty of land travel before trails were improved into crude roads.

- Major Danforth, who settled at Onondaga Hill in 1788, traveled 40 miles on foot to Utica to obtain a saw for his sawmill and returned the 40 miles with it on his back.

- Benjamin Morehouse carried a plowshare, to be sharpened by a blacksmith, 30 miles each way from Manlius to Westmoreland.

- When Cyrus Kinne, his wife and four sons came from Eastern New York to DeWitt in 1792, after passing Oneida, they had to cut roads and fell trees to make bridges over streams for their ox team and horse.

- The first settlers in Clay had to carry their grain over 12 miles to Jamesville to have it ground, and then carry the grist back home.

We can only imagine how important the improvement of trails into passable roads was to the early settlers. Primitive roads made it possible to transport needed items from place to place, move farm products to market and opened the lands of Central New York to thousands of new settlers. It took many years but, step by step, roads were laid out, cut through the forests and gradually improved to provide for the needs of a growing population.

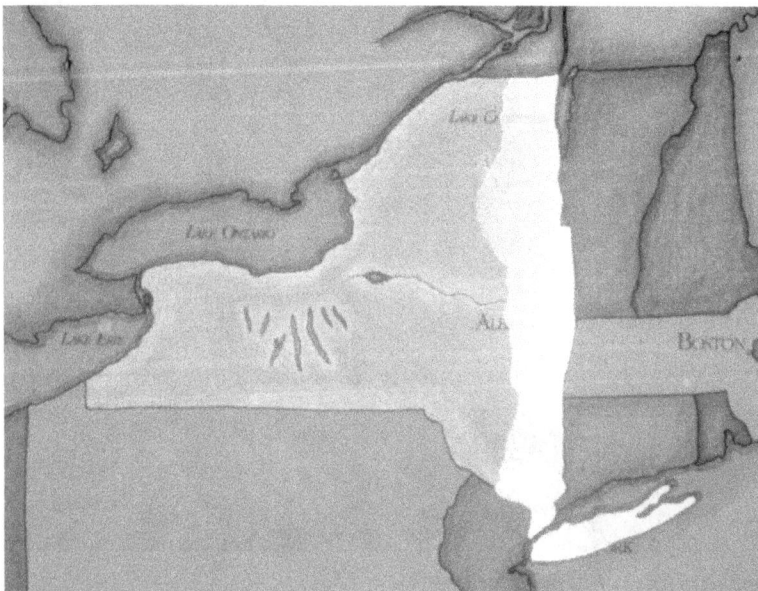

A map of New York State at the end of the Revolutionary War. The light area, consisting of Long Island, the Hudson River Valley, the Champlain Valley and a narrow strip along the Mohawk River Valley was all that had been settled. The remainder of the state was rapidly settled during the next 50 years.

CHAPTER 2

Major Early Central New York Roads

As we travel daily on the fine highways of today, almost no one gives any thought to the early history of roads. This chapter relates some of the history of what transpired when road construction and maintenance were in their infancy. The past 80 years will be largely ignored even though great strides in road construction and maintenance have occurred. These recent changes are well recorded but, other than divided major highways, seem less dramatic than the changes made from the time of Native American footpaths of 1600 to the concrete highways of the 1920s.

It is a common misconception that the majority of today's highways follow the trails made by Native Americans centuries ago. Portions of some of our major highways do follow those trails but the majority of our country roads were trails made by white men as they traveled from their homes to the nearest hamlet or to their neighbors' homes. With farm size averaging a little under 100 acres at the time Central New York was settled, roads needed to be within a mile of each other so that each farm had access to a roadway. From this there developed a system of roadways far more extensive than the trails used by the Native Americans whose population was much smaller and lived in small villages rather than in homes scattered over the countryside.

The white man's road system had its beginning in Central New York with the founding of Oswego. The Mohawk River, Wood Creek, Oneida Lake and the Oneida and Oswego Rivers provided waterways for trade and travel from the Mohawk Valley to Oswego, but a road for travel on land was also desired. In 1756, Sir William Johnson, who served as Superintendent of Indian Affairs for the British, obtained permission from the Oneida, Tuscarora and Onondaga Indians to build a road from German Flats, about 15 miles east of Utica near Herkimer, to Oswego. This road followed a westerly direction crossing Chittenango Creek and then crossing the Seneca River south of Three Rivers Point. It then headed north along the western shore of the Oswego

River to Lake Ontario. The Indians participated in the road's construction as it passed through their respective territories. It was a rough, primitive road and would have had numerous sections of corduroy (trees laid side by side covered with a thin layer of dirt) as it passed through wet lands.[1]

An indication of the difficulty of early travel across New York State is provided by Dr. Jeremy Belknap who kept a written account of his trip from Boston to Niagara in 1796, to inspect a Mission established among the Oneida Indians. Dr. Belknap had the means to pay whatever was necessary and traveled with little luggage, which was in marked contrast to settlers coming to upstate New York. Following are some excerpts from his diary:

One day from Albany to Schenectady, 16 miles; next day by stage to Canajoharie, 40 miles; third day by stage to Whitestown where the stage ends, 46 miles; fourth day by hired wagon to Fort Stanwix, 12 miles; fifth day portage to Wood Creek, 2 miles; sixth day by water down Wood Creek to Oneida Lake, 27 miles; seventh day across Oneida Lake to Fort Bruington (Fort at Brewerton) 35 miles; eighth day down the river to Oswego Falls (Fulton), 12 miles; ninth day portage of 150 feet and then to Oswego Fort on Lake Ontario, 12 miles; then on Lake Ontario to Niagara.[2]

An article by Benjamin DeWitt, published in the *Transactions of the Society for the Promotion of Useful Arts* in 1807 provides his view, and quite likely the view of most New York leaders in 1807, of the importance of roads to the advancement of civilization.

"The progress of improvements in public highways, turnpike roads, bridges and canals, has ever been considered an interesting subject. There is an inseparable

---

1   Beauchamp, Rev. William M. *Past and Present of Syracuse and Onondaga County* p. 240
2   Hedrick, Ulysses Prentiss *A History of Agriculture in the State of New York* p. 167

Section of Map made in 1792 by
Simeon DeWitt, Surveyor-General of the State of New York

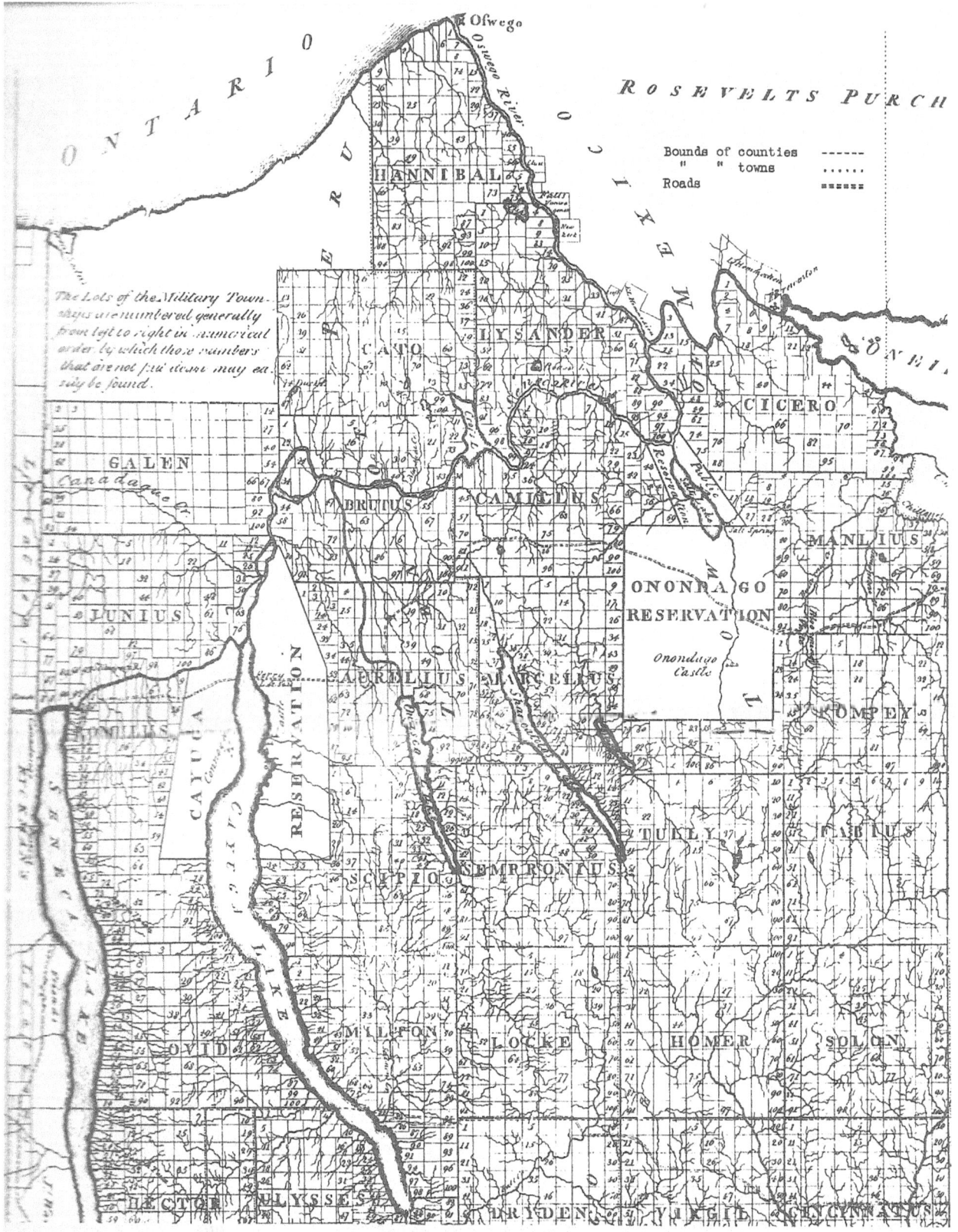

A 1792 map showing the Military Tract. Each little square, consisting of approximately 600 acres, was given to certain Revolutionary War soldiers from New York State. Roads were gradually cut through the forests within about two little squares of each other, sometimes closer and sometimes further apart, depending upon the terrain.

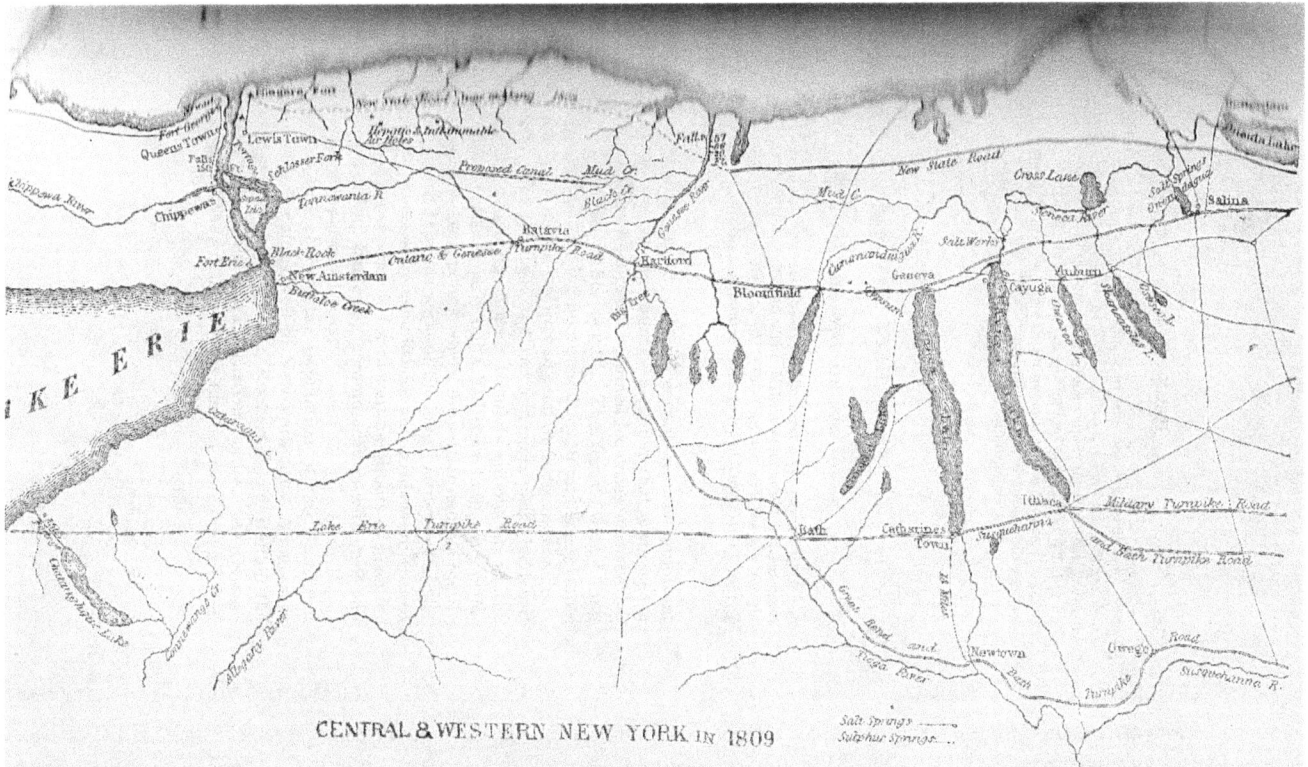

A 1809 map of Western New York showing some of the major roads and turnpikes at that time.

connection between these, and the agriculture, arts and commerce of a country. The condition of the former is a criterion to the advancement of the latter. The one is a natural and a necessary consequence of the other. Where there is no agriculture, there are no roads; and without roads there can be but little commerce: Hence the existence of roads has been considered a line of demarkation, between the civilized and the savage state. And hence also the excellence of public highways, marks the the degree of general improvements in a country. Thus the rude essays of the early Peruvians, in constructing their celebrated great roads, has contributed to rank them amongst the civilized, instead of the savage nations: And thus the beauty and perfection of the famous Roman highways, characterized the flourishing state of that empire. Thus also in our own country the contrast between our present turnpike roads, and the dismal footpaths of the aborigines, is not greater, than between our state of civilization and refinement, and their condition of rudeness and barbarity."

Money to build early roads came from a variety of sources. Both the United States and New York State were young, having been formed only two or three decades before the need arose for roads in Central New York. The Revolutionary War had left both the federal and the state governments in debt requiring money for road improvements to come from other sources. New York State held lotteries to raise money. It sold some of the land taken from the Native Americans around Onondaga Lake as well as land in the Military Tract that was not assigned to Revolutionary veterans. (The military grants were divided into approximately 600 acre parcels. If the recipient had received 100 acres in Ohio from the federal government, he received only 500 acres in his New York grant with the remaining becoming known as "the State's one hundred acres.") New York also assessed eligible males a minimum of three days of road work a year, which could be avoided by paying a fee of 62.5 cents a day.[3] The largest source of money for roads came from private enterprise. The State granted companies the right to collect tolls from the users of roads and bridges for a specific number of years, if certain requirements were met in their construction. Often these investors purchased land in proximity to a proposed turnpike and

3   Klein, Daniel B., Santa Clara University & Majewski, John, University of California-Santa Barbara *Turnpikes and Toll Roads in Nineteenth -Century America*

A turnpike tollgate on the Manlius Oran Road circa 1899. Many of New York's early major roads were constructed by investors hoping to make a profit from the tolls collected. Courtesy of the OHA Museum & Research Center

reaped large rewards because of the increased value of the land near a road. Later, as counties and towns began to become populated and a tax base developed, these local jurisdictions started assessing real estate taxes to pay for roads. In later paragraphs you will find that road taxes were not always paid with money.

An increasing number of settlers heading west from Albany and Utica required more and better roads. In Benjamin DeWitt's article cited earlier he comments on the magnitude of road building in the new State of New York since 1800. He lists 88 incorporated turnpike road and bridge companies with a total capital of more than $5.5 million, covering more than 3,000 miles of roads and requiring building of 20 large toll bridges. Among the many listed were Seneca Turnpike, consisting of two roads covering 112 miles with capital stock of $180,000; Onondaga Salt Spring Turnpike, 55 miles with capital of $100,000; and the Hamilton and Skaneateles Turnpike, 70 miles with capital of $80,000.[4]

Turnpikes became prominent in England during what was known as 'Turnpike Mania' from 1750 to 1772. The first turnpike in the United States was chartered in

Pennsylvania in 1792. By 1800 there were 13 turnpikes chartered in New York, increasing to 339 by 1830. Turnpikes represented 34% of all New York corporations formed between 1800 and 1830 and the money expended was more than 7% of New York's domestic gross product. New York required inspection and approval of a minimum of 10 miles before permission was granted to charge tolls. As a result, and because the average cost was over $1,500 a mile, only about 165 reached operational status.[5]

Cayuga Bridge, constructed in 1797 where the Seneca Turnpike crossed the north end of Cayuga Lake, was an engineering marvel. The bridge was more than a mile long and was 22 feet wide with 22 feet between each trestle. It was constructed in 18 months and cost $150,000. Many thousands of settlers and travelers crossed this bridge, which at the time was considered the dividing line between east and west in New York State. The nearby Montezuma Marshes made travel north of the lake virtually impossible and the bridge eliminated the need of a ferry to cross the lake. The bridge burned

4   Hedrick, Uylsses Prentiss *A History of Agriculture in the State of New York* p. 168-170

5   Klein, Daniel B., Santa Clara University & Majewski, John, University of California-Santa Barbara *Turnpikes and Toll Roads in Nineteenth-Century America*

in 1804, was rebuilt in 1812 and abandoned in 1857.[6]

The first road to cross Onondaga County was what later became known as the Great Genesee Road. Around 1790 a party of emigrants led by General Wadsworth cut a road through land that was little explored and virtually wilderness from Whitestown (slightly west of Utica) to Canandaigua, a distance of over 100 miles. On the east it crossed the Onondaga County line a little north of Deep Spring (approximately where Route 173 crosses from Madison County into Onondaga County), passing through today's Manlius village, crossing Butternut Creek a mile south of Jamesville, through Onondaga Hollow to near General Hutchinson's home about a mile west of Onondaga Hill, on what is now Route 175. After

this road was cut through the forests, traffic of settlers heading west greatly increased. As early as 1800, the settlements along this road from Utica to Canandaigua attained some consequence.[7] The route from Deep Spring to Onondaga Hollow was almost the same as the Indian trail of 1756.[8]

In 1793, John L. Hardenburgh, Moses De Witt and John Patterson were appointed to the newly created Board of Commissioners for laying out and opening public roads in the Military Tract, of which the current Onondaga County is a part. The principal road passed from the Deep Spring to the Cayuga Ferry with others located in different parts of the Military Tract. The roads were

---

6 Hedrick, Ulysses Prentiss *A History of Agriculture in the State of New York* p. 177-178

7 Clark, Joshua V.H. *Onondaga* p.383
8 Beauchamp, Rev. William M. *Past and Present of Syracuse and Onondaga County New York* p. 241

Comfort Tyler's Tavern at Onondaga Hill in the early 1800s. Notice the stagecoach with passengers in front of the tavern and the team of oxen and oxcart in the background. Taverns similar to this one were located every few miles along the turnpikes to accommodate travelers.

to be laid out four rods wide (66 feet) and the sum of $2,700 was appropriated for that purpose.[9]

Joshua Clark provides detailed descriptions of the early roads in Central New York in his book *Onondaga*, published in 1849, as follows:

"In 1794 an act was passed by the legislature of the State of New York appointing Israel Chapin, Michael Myers and Orthniel Taylor, commissioners for the purpose of laying out, and improving a public highway, from Old Fort Schuyler, on the Mohawk River to the Cayuga Ferry, as nearly straight as the situation of the country would allow. Thence from Cayuga Ferry to Canandaigua, and thence to the settlement of Canawagas (Avon), on the Genesee River. Road to be six rods wide (99 feet) and the sum of 600 pounds (approximately $3000) was appropriated for the expense of opening and improving so much of the road as passed through the Military Tract. In 1796, the Surveyor General was authorized to sell certain lands on the Indian Reservation, and from the proceeds of the sales, appropriate 500 pounds for improving the Great Genesee Road through the County of Onondaga."

Another act passed by the legislature in 1796 was the appointment of Seth Williams, William Stevens and Comfort Tyler as commissioners to make and repair the highways of Onondaga County. The legislature appropriated $4,000 and directed that half of the money was to be used to improve the portion of the Great Genesee Road that passed through Onondaga County. This money was to come from surplus from the sale of State lots in the various towns. The following year the New York Legislature authorized three lotteries to raise $45,000 for the further improvement of roads and specified that $13,900 of it was to be used to improve the Great Genesee Road from Old Fort Schuyler to Geneva.[10]

A letter written by Captain Charles Williamson, an agent for English owners of lands in 'Genesee Country', written in the later part of 1797, shows the need and effectiveness of the appropriations by the State for road improvements.

"By this generous and uncommon exertion, and by some other contributions, the State Commissioner was able to complete this road of near 100 miles, opening it 64 feet wide, and paving with logs and gravel, the moist parts of the low country. Hence the road from Fort Schuyler on the Mohawk River, to Genesee, from being in the month of June 1797, little better than an Indian path, was so far improved, that a stage started

---

9 Clark, Joshua V.H. *Onondaga* p. 384

10 Clark, Joshua V.H. *Onondaga* p.385

This photo shows the hazards of driving on many country roads in the early 1900s. The speed bumps came as a natural part of the road.

from Fort Schuyler on the 30th day of September, and arrived at the hotel in Geneva, in the afternoon of the third day, with four passengers. This line of road having been established by law, not less than 50 families settled on it in the space of four months after it was opened."[11]

In 1800, the Seneca Road Company was granted a charter by the Legislature authorizing it to improve the old State Road, which in Onondaga County passed through Manlius, Jamesville, Onondaga Valley and Marcellus, now a combination of Routes 173 and 175. The capital stock of the Company was originally $110,000 but was increased by another $50,000 later. In 1801, an amendment to the charter gave the company some discretionary right to deviate from the old road. When a number of residents living along the old road heard this they, through devious means, prevailed upon the company to maintain the same route as the old road. In 1806, when the Seneca Road Company discovered they had been misled, they secured a further amendment to their charter authorizing them to build a new road from Sullivan to the Onondaga Reservation, near the Salt Springs to Cayuga Bridge. This new road was finished in 1812 and was known as the North Branch of the Seneca Road, but was later called the Genesee Turnpike. The road passed through Fayetteville, Syracuse, Camillus and on to the West.[12] (Later this road became Route 5.)

The importance of these new and improved roads cannot be over emphasized. Until the opening of the Erie Canal, in 1825, thousands of people made the westward trek on these roadways to settle in Central and Western New York, as well as states further west. Merchandise to supply these new settlers traveled along the same roads in a westerly direction while salt, wheat and other products produced here traveled east to distant markets. These roads were also important for the movement of mail. In 1797-8 the mail was carried on horseback. Later it was carried by horse and wagon. The first four-horse mail coach was established in 1804 and made one trip weekly from Utica to Canandaigua. In 1805, the State Legislature granted Jason Parker and Levi Stevens the right to run stages between Utica and Canandaigua for seven years with the requirements of two trips a week with a maximum of 48 hours, accidents excepted, and with a maximum passenger fare of five cents a mile. By 1808, stages were running daily.[13]

There were several other roads of varying importance authorized by the State and opened in Onondaga County before the War of 1812. In 1806, State legislation appropriated $600 from duties on salt to improve the road along the northeast shore of Onondaga Lake, a road much used for the transport of salt. In 1807, the Surveyor General directed that a six rod road (99 feet

11 Bruce, Dwight H. *Onondaga's Centennial* p. 198-199
12 Bruce, Dwight H. *Onondaga's Centennial* p. 199

13 Bruce, Dwight H. *Onondaga's Centennial* p. 199-200

Springtime on a country road. It recalls a common expression of the time used by passing farmers driving a horse and wagon, and exclaiming, "Get a horse!"

wide) be laid out north and south from the Walton Tract on State lands. (The Walton Tract was where the center of Syracuse is now located and a part of this road became Salina Street.) Also in 1807, the Chenango and Salina Turnpike Co. was authorized to build a good road from Salina (now the center of Syracuse) south through Onondaga to the North line of the Town of Tully and southward from there. (This would correspond with current Route 11.) In 1806, an east to west road was laid out from Richfield through Brookfield, Hamilton, Fabius and Marietta to Skaneateles. [14] (Currently this is much of Route 80.)

Another early road of short-lived prominence was designated by New York State to be laid out in the most direct way from the bridge over Sodus Bay to the new bridge, (Snow's Bridge), over the Seneca River at Adam's Ferry (near the end of Tator Rd. at its intersection with Plainville Rd.) and from there to Onondaga Hill. The road from Onondaga Hill to Snow's Bridge crossing the Seneca River had been established at an earlier date with the Adams family operating a ferry for crossing the river until Snow's bridge was constructed in 1810 by the Towns of Camillus (Van Buren was part of Camillus then) and Lysander at a cost of $750.[15] Snow's Bridge had only a 19 year life and was dismantled when a new bridge was constructed over the Seneca River at Jack's Reef, about two miles further south.

The earliest roads had no bridges to cross rivers and streams. Originally the roads headed toward a spot on the rivers where access in and out was relatively easy and where there were rifts to provide shallower water. One example was in Baldwinsville where a road coming from the south went straight down to the Seneca River and crossed in a northeasterly direction, at the rifts a bit north of the current dam. In 1807, after Jonas Baldwin constructed a dam across the river, he built a toll bridge across the river and the days of fording the river ended.[16]

New York State had a very limited amount of money available to construct highways. As a result, companies were formed to construct highways over a specific route and collect tolls for a certain number of years to cover their expenses and hopefully return a profit to company investors. By 1813, there had been 180 turnpike companies incorporated in New York State.

Dwight H. Bruce, in his book *Onondaga's Centennial*, lists the companies whose roads passed into or through Onondaga County as follows:

The First Northern Company, incorporated April 1, 1799; the Great Northern Company, incorporated April 4, 1805; the Great Western Company, incorporated, March 15, 1799; the Second Great Western Company, incorporated April 4, 1801; the Third Great Western Company, incorporated April 4, 1803, the Fourth Great Western Company, incorporated March 28, 1805; the Manlius and Truxton, incorporated April 9, 1811; the Military Road, April 6, 1808; the Onondaga Salt Spring Company, incorporated April 4, 1805; the Salina and Chenango Company, incorporated April 6, 1807; the Seneca Turnpike Company, incorporated April 1, 1800. The Skaneateles Turnpike Company was incorporated in February 1813, and the time for the construction of their road was afterwards extended to 1817.

Each of the major roads constructed by these companies attracted settlers to the countryside for miles around as well as along the roads themselves. They were the arteries of Onondaga County, which spawned many of our present day villages and the industries that developed within them.

An interesting consequence of the effect of the opening of the Erie Canal's middle section upon turnpikes running parallel to the Canal is related in a May 5,1823 article in the *Onondaga Register*. It stated that with the opening of the middle section of the Erie Canal, paralleling the Seneca Turnpike, teams of six and eight horses pulling heavy wagons were almost totally removed from the Turnpike and road repairs were greatly decreased.

As more remote areas of the County were settled and as the population increased throughout the County, additional roads were constructed. The Syracuse and Tully Turnpike Company was incorporated on April 25,1831 to construct a turnpike from the Hamilton and Skaneateles Turnpike in Tully to Syracuse and to charge tolls. There were 1,000 shares of stock issued at $20 each. Incorporated on April, 23, 1831 was the Syracuse and Pulaski Turnpike Company and on April 24, 1831, the Salina and Oswego Turnpike Company.[17]

---

17 Bruce, Dwight H. *Onondaga's Centennial* p. 230

---

14 Bruce, Dwight H. *Onondaga's Centennial* p. 200
15 Palmer, Pearl *Historical Review of the Town of Lysander* Part 47
16 Bruce, Dwight H. *Onondaga's Centennial* p. 720

First Plank Rd. in the U.S. 1846-1913
Present day Rt. 11 Salina, Mattydale, No. Syracuse, Cicero
and Central Square

This is a photograph of the first plank road in America, constructed in 1846 between Salina and Central Square. There was at least one plank road in Baldwinsville and one that extended from the village west to Emerick Road. The planks wore out quickly and the plank road era lasted only a few decades. Courtesy of Mr. & Mrs. Harold Baker

The following quotes from M.C. Hand's book, *From a Forest to a City*, written in 1889 of his personal reminiscences of Syracuse, New York provide a vivid idea of the conditions of streets in Syracuse in its early years. The conditions described were not very different from those on many of the roads in Lysander and Van Buren or even Baldwinsville in the spring of the year or after heavy rains.

"Much of the central portion of the city was originally a swamp, and when the water was drained off, the ground was still soft so much that every foot of Genesee St. to the higher lands on the east were first paved with logs of wood to keep the horses and wagons from miring in the soft soil."

"At one time it was impossible to make the trip from Onondaga Valley to Salina over the road that is now Salina St. before June as the roadway made of brush and logs was under water until that time."

"Kirk's Tavern, built on the corner of Fayette and Salina Streets in 1826, and other boarding houses in the vicinity were seldom patronized by boarders on account of the mud encountered in going to and from their meals."

"Syracuse sometimes was called the 'City of Mud'."

Fewer new roads were surveyed and constructed after 1850 other than in the towns close to Syracuse, such as Salina, Geddes and Onondaga where there were greater increases in population. Canals and railroads helped minimize the use of roads for long distance transportation, whereas a growing city population put greater demands upon roads in heavily populated areas. Plank roads served as a short term solution to this problem.

In 1846, the first plank road, of which there were later hundreds in the United States, was constructed from Salina (now Syracuse) to Central Square, a distance of 16.5 miles. This was a highly traveled road with barrels of salt heading north and empty barrels heading south to the salt works at Salina, along with all sorts of other merchandise traveling in both directions. The plank road was viewed as a great improvement over the existing roads which were often barely passable during the spring and fall because of mud and deep ruts. A grand celebration was held at its opening with a procession over its length and speeches by area dignitaries. The road consisted of three inch planks eight feet long, providing sufficient width for only one vehicle and requiring vehicles with lighter loads to pull off the planks when meeting vehicles with heavier loads. These roads became the rage with plank roads constructed from Syracuse south to Cortland, north to Oswego, west to Elbridge, east to Manlius and numerous others of shorter distances and of lesser importance in the area.

There was also a double wide plank road constructed in Syracuse on Warren Street allowing two meeting vehicles to both stay on the road. An important item overlooked in the construction of these plank roads was their short life, due to wear from the wagon wheels and the deterioration of the wood due to the elements. Another factor leading to their demise was the increased use of railroads for shipment of freight, reducing toll income on the plank roads. Although initially many had been profitable because of their extensive use, later plank roads became too expensive to maintain and gradually went out of existence.[18] Baldwinsville, like many other communities, had some plank roads for short periods of time as noted in the next chapter.

---

18 Bruce, Dwight H. *Onondaga's Centennial* p. 236-7

CHAPTER 3

Baldwinsville Area Roads and Bridges

A complete account of local road and bridge history would be a thick and boring book. A few examples, as our roads developed from the beginning of our municipalities until the 1930s, are provided to give the reader some indication of the process taking place. Much of the information in this section came directly from the official records of the towns of Lysander and Van Buren.

Louis Dow Scisco in his book, *Early History of the Town of Van Buren*, written in 1895, refers to an old Indian trail through Dead Creek Valley in his description of early roads.

"No regular roads existed in the town for many years after settlement began. The old trail through the Dead Creek Valley was used by the more northern settlers to go southward, while forest paths crossing the town from cabin to cabin availed for neighborly communication. Along these paths the settler paced with gun in hand, keeping a wary eye for any passing wild beast."

Since travel by white settlers was first on foot and later with oxen or horses, roads avoided the steepest hills and wet lands, often meandering across the countryside. These early roads followed the paths of least resistance and often make the drivers of today's powerful and much faster vehicles wonder as to the sobriety of their designers.

The majority of our area's roads had very simple beginnings. Paths passing from house to house

This photograph, circa 1870, is looking north on Syracuse and Oswego Streets. In the background, on the left, is the spire of the present Presbyterian Church, built in 1865. On the right, at 50 Oswego St., is Herrick's Hall, which had been the Presbyterian Church before it was sold and moved. The large building across the river on the left is the Miller knitting mill and the large white building across the river on the right is the Amos flour mill.

ALBANY & BETHLEHEM TURNPIKE ROAD.
RATES OF TOLL.

FOR EVERY SCORE OF SHEEP OR HOGS,	6 Cents.
FOR EVERY SCORE OF CATTLE, HORSES OR MULES,	15 Cents.
& So in proportion for a greater or less number of SHEEP, HOGS, CATTLE, HORSES OR MULES,	
FOR EVERY SULKY, CHAISE OR CHAIR WITH ONE HORSE, 12½ Cents. N.B. For this item, instead of the LEGAL TOLL the Company accepts,	4 Cents.
FOR EVERY CART DRAWN BY ONE HORSE,	4 Cents
FOR EVERY CHARIOT, COACH, COACHEE OR PHAETON, DRAWN BY TWO HORSES, 19 Cents, N.B. For this item, instead of the LEGAL TOLL, the Company accepts	12½ Cents.
& Two Cents for every additional Horse,	
FOR EVERY COVERED STAGE WAGON, DRAWN BY 2 HORSES, 12½ Cents. N.B. For this item, instead the LEGAL TOLL, the Company accepts	6 Cents.
and 2 cents for every additional Horse,	
FOR EVERY OTHER WAGON, DRAWN BY 2 HORSES, MULES OR OXEN, and 2 Cents for every additional Horse, Mule or Ox.	6 Cents.
FOR EVERY CART DRAWN BY 2 HORSES, MULES OR OXEN, and 2 Cents for every additional Horse, Mule or Ox.	6 Cents
FOR EVERY ONE HORSE WAGON DRAWN BY ONE HORSE.	5 Cents
FOR EVERY SLEIGH OR SLED, DRAWN BY 2 HORSES, MULES OR and 2 Cent for each additional Horse, Mule or Ox. OXEN.	6 Cents
FOR EVERY ONE HORSE SLEIGH,	4 Cents
FOR EVERY HORSE & RIDER,	4 Cents
FOR EVERY LED HORSE,	2 Cents

A rate of toll sign, although not from Baldwinsville, showing tolls similar to those charged by Dr. Baldwin for crossing the Seneca River over his bridge from 1809 to 1837. Courtesy of Albany Institute of History & Art, u1972.16.1

constructed in 1809. It was specified that it be not less than 20 feet wide and that he could collect tolls for 30 years, according to the following rates: every two-horse carriage paid 20 cents, a two-horse wagon 15 cents, a mounted rider eight cents and a person on foot four cents. Domestic animals in herds or droves were also taxed when crossing the bridge.[1] This road was improved in 1814 making it friendlier to the stagecoaches, wagons and carriages that were becoming more common. Some people who were continual users of the bridge paid a yearly fee in advance. Mrs. H.B. Allen noted, in the 50th Anniversary publication of *The Gazette and Farmers' Journal* of 1896, that she possessed two documents relating to Baldwin's toll bridge. One was a notice to the toll keeper to let Philip Sharp pass over the bridge without charge from the first day of March in 1827 to the first day of March in 1828. The other was also for Sharp, allowing him passage without toll between March 1,1831 and March 1, 1832.

eventually became roads laid out and surveyed by towns. Early roads in Baldwinsville also were laid out and surveyed by the encompassing town. Two examples in the Lysander portion of the village are Charlotte Street, which was laid out and surveyed in 1833, and Gaston Street, now East Genesee from Salina St. east to New Bridge (Belgium) in 1832.

In 1807, a road was laid out from Onondaga Hill to Ox Creek in the Town of Granby in Oswego County and from there on to Oswego. It was the first major road passing through Baldwinsville. Originally this road passed through what is now Riverview Cemetery and crossed the river at the head of the rifts near the end of North St. The change in its path, when it was laid out through Dr. Jonas Baldwin's land holdings was likely due to his influence. On April 7, 1807, the State empowered him to build a bridge over the Seneca River, which was

Road districts were established and an overseer or path master was appointed who determined when road work was to be done. Residents in each district were assigned a number of days work on the road depending upon the valuation of their property. It was a tax paid with labor rather than with money. For example, in the Town of Lysander, there were 13 road districts in 1811, becoming 24 in 1814, 39 in 1825, 66 in 1835, 91 in 1860 and reaching 100 road districts in 1880. In 1818, the inhabitants of the Town of Lysander were assessed a total of 974 days work on the roads.[2] Part of the increase in the number of road districts was because of additional roads but also because residents desired more improvements to the roads, requiring more districts and taking a greater number of days to make improvements on each mile of roads.

1   Scisco, Louis Dow *Early History of the Town of Van Buren* P. 25
2   Bruce, Dwight H. *Onondaga's Centennial* p. 754

The number of days required varied from year to year but a resolution passed by the Lysander Town Board on March 18, 1884, offers an insight about the method used to determine the number of days a land owner was required to work on the roads. It stated that the basis of labor for highway work was to be one day of work for each $800 of assessment or by a fraction of $200.

Road work similar to Lysander's existed throughout Central New York. The tools available for the road work in the early 1800s were very simple, perhaps a shovel, crowbar, hoe and axe. The work involved the use of oxen and consisted of removing fallen trees and large boulders besides filling the deepest ruts with stones. The country roads of the early 1800s bore no resemblance to the roads that exist today. As a community developed travel on the roads increased, roads gradually were improved and varied forms of vehicles used them.

The road district overseer, often called path master, 'ordered the farmers out' in the spring of the year after the early farm work had been completed, to fulfill their obligation of work in their respective road district. Later in the 19th century, road work, other than bridges and culverts for drainage, was performed by men with teams of horses pulling wagons that had been loaded by hand with dirt, gravel or stone, depending upon what was readily available. Ruts in the roads were filled and leveled, and low areas of the road were corduroyed or filled with stone and covered with gravel.

Highway laws of the 1800s sometimes permitted the road tax to be satisfied in ways other than just a specified number of days. One option was planting shade trees along the roadway to ease travel for both man and beast in hot weather. Another way was to furnish a water trough with a source of water to provide thirsty oxen and horses with a drink while yet another choice was to furnish a team and wagon for road repair. Freezing and thawing during the winter along with heavy rains assured that the taxpayers would be assigned highway work each year. Rural roads and village streets had dirt and gravel surfaces while side roads were natural earth with mud holes filled with stones and gravel.[3]

---

3   Christopher, A.J. *Pathmasters Care for Early Roads*, The *Baldwinsville Messenger*, April 1, 1965

This picture shows the tollgate on State Fair Blvd. with the Syracuse, Lakeside and Baldwinsville trolley tracks passing in the foreground. This would have been one of the last tollgates constructed in the area before the New York State Thruway tollgates in the 1950s.

After roads were laid out and surveyed on the virgin soils in the newly formed community of Columbia (Baldwinsville), buildings were constructed along these pathways. Soon, and continually over the years, roads in the village were improved with gravel, corduroy or planks.

Canal Street in Baldwinsville was laid out by 1810 but was little more than natural earth at the time. Later it was improved to a corduroy street from the Methodist Church to the Salina St. intersection. A corduroy road is useful in a wet area that is heavily traveled. Trees are laid side by side and then covered with dirt and gravel to provide a rough but sturdy surface for wagons and other vehicles. Canal St. was probably made corduroy because of the many heavy loads of logs coming to the Baldwin sawmill. Another village corduroy road extended from the four-corners up the Oswego St. hill.

Canal St. received a great deal of use and in 1837 the Baldwinsville Plank Road Company was formed to improve it from the east end of Charlotte St., across the four-corners to the top of Holland's Hill, across from the present brewery. Sawed planks were used and a tollgate was placed on each end of the road. The plank road was used for 20 years with the owners surrendering their franchise in 1857.[4]

The extent of road improvements is difficult to comprehend until one reads an article in the 50th Anniversary publication of *The Gazette and Farmers'*

4   Christopher, A.J. *Village Once Had Streets of Planks, The Baldwinsville Messenger*, March 30, 1967

Journal, published in 1896, about the American Hotel. The hotel was located on the northeast corner of the intersection of Bridge and Canal Streets (now Oswego and E. Genesee Streets). The first building, which later became part of the hotel, was constructed in 1814. The hotel opened in 1831 and continued in use until 1899 when it was destroyed by fire. The article stated that the hotel had been raised nine feet, over the years, to keep pace with the elevation of the street! It is hard to imagine the need to raise a building that much. The article also mentioned that the road had initially been six rods wide but was later changed to four rods (66 feet).

Lysander Roads

The book, *Survey of Roads, 1805-1894, of the Town of Lysander*, along with the town meeting records provide many interesting insights into the development of the town's road system. Applications by individual land owners for laying out a highway to fill a specific landowner's need were often recorded. An application for a new road needed to be signed by 12 respectable free holders of the town certifying that the road was necessary and proper to be laid out. Next, the Lysander Commissioners of Highways deliberated and if they determined it was needed, the road was laid out and a survey made.

Occasionally a proposed road passed through the farm of a person that didn't want the road. A specific case, recorded in 1839, covered three handwritten pages in Lysander's Survey of Roads Book. Clarence Bayley, a land owner whose property was being divided by a

A circa 1930 photograph of downtown Baldwinsville looking north on Oswego Street. The street is greatly improved, paved with brick and sidewalks made of concrete.

A circa 1925 photograph of a new concrete road being constructed. Workers put sand, crushed stone and cement into the mixer which dumped the concrete on the other side where it was leveled for the new highway. The concrete mixer was pulled ahead, a few feet at a time, as the road was formed. Photo courtesy of the OHA Museum & Research Center.

proposed road, appealed the laying out of a new road and went before a panel of justices for their decision. Clarence Bayley lost his case but was entitled to damages. Apparently he wasn't satisfied with the amount of damages so he appealed and the Lysander justices ordered that a constable in the neighboring Town of Van Buren summon 12 disinterested freeholders in the Town of Van Buren, that were not kin to Clarence, to meet in the Town of Lysander and specify the damages sustained by Clarence by the road going through his property. After hearing the case the 12 freeholders awarded Clarence $75. In this case the constable's fee was $2, the two justices each received $2, the 12 jurors received a total of $9 and the Lysander Road Commissioners $2 making a total cost of the proceedings $17. No indication was given whether Clarence was happy or not but he had certainly been provided with a fair opportunity for justice. In most cases residents wanted the roads so litigation like Clarence's was rare.

The initial survey of the original roads did not always reflect the actual path of the roads. Perhaps road use did not exactly follow the paths of the original surveys or, with time, the paths adopted by vehicles occasionally deviated to provide greater ease of travel by avoiding a steep portion of a hill or a wet area. In 1843, there was a resurvey of approximately 50 Town of Lysander roads. One of the roads with a resurvey extended the length of the Town from the Cayuga County line to the Cold Springs bridge, now Route 370. No mention was made as to the changes that may have been necessary to this or any other road.

On page 286, in the Lysander book of highways, is an 1811 survey of the road from Baldwinsville to the Cold Spring Bridge over the Seneca River, as copied from the original survey by Lysander Town Clerk, Gertrude Kratzer on April 10, 1942. A few words are missing because of the age of the document, and the author intentionally omitted the various degrees and distances. It stated:

"Survey of a publick highway laid from the village of Columbia to the Seneca River below the Cold Spring in the Town of Lysander. Beginning at village lots No. 146 & 147 thence North 75 degrees East (skip) to a stake on the bank of the Seneca River (skip) thence down the river (skip) to a stake near the bank of the Seneca River (skip) being in the whole length, four miles and 32 rods. Surveyed 6 Oct. 1811 by Henry B. Turner."

At the annual Town Meeting held in and for the Town of Lysander on the seventh day of April 1840, at the Seneca Hotel in the Village of Baldwinsville the overseers of the 74 highway districts for 1840 were named along with the number of days of roadwork to be completed in each District. The number of days required varied from nine in District 47 to 109 in District 3. Nothing is stated regarding the criteria used in determining the number of days work required or the length of the day or if a team of oxen counted as an additional day.

One of the many plank roads in Onondaga County was along the Seneca River west from Baldwinsville, following the path of current Route 370. On page 75 in the Lysander roads record is its survey. A summary of the survey follows. *Beginning at the intersection of the North side of the Syracuse and Oswego Railroad and the center line of Gaston Street (now Route 31 to Belgium) in the village of Baldwinsville, continuing West through Baldwinsville on West Genesee Street to Emerick Road and beyond, making a total distance of 249 chains and 62 links.* (a little over 3.1 miles) It also stated that the width was to be one chain. (66 feet) The Lysander Highway Commissioners ordered that the survey be recorded and this occurred on July 24, 1848.

An examination of the book of the Town of Lysander records from 1836 to 1893 gives us a view of the extent of work on roads and bridges in the Town during that time. In 1839, the Lysander Town Commissioner of roads and bridges stated that the roads and bridges were out of repair and that $150 needed to be raised to repair them that year. By 1845, the amount that needed to be raised had increased to $200 and by 1850 the sum of $250 was needed. Plank replacement on bridges was an ongoing annual cost and as the bridges aged more plank needed to be replaced.

A sign that Lysander was maturing is evident in an April 6, 1841 resolution stating that no cattle or hogs 'shall run at large' on the highway within one mile of any tavern, store or grist mill under the penalty of $5 for each offense. This was a serious fine as it represented more than the average man's weekly wage. In 1836, the Town decreed that every path master (road overseer) was to also be a pound master and fence viewer and that his yard was to serve as the pound, which meant that any loose animal in violation of the law would be held by the pound master until the fine had been paid.

Lysander records show that the road districts were often changed, sometimes combining districts and at other times making two districts from one. In addition, specific plots of land were moved from one road district to another. For example changes decreed by the Town of Lysander

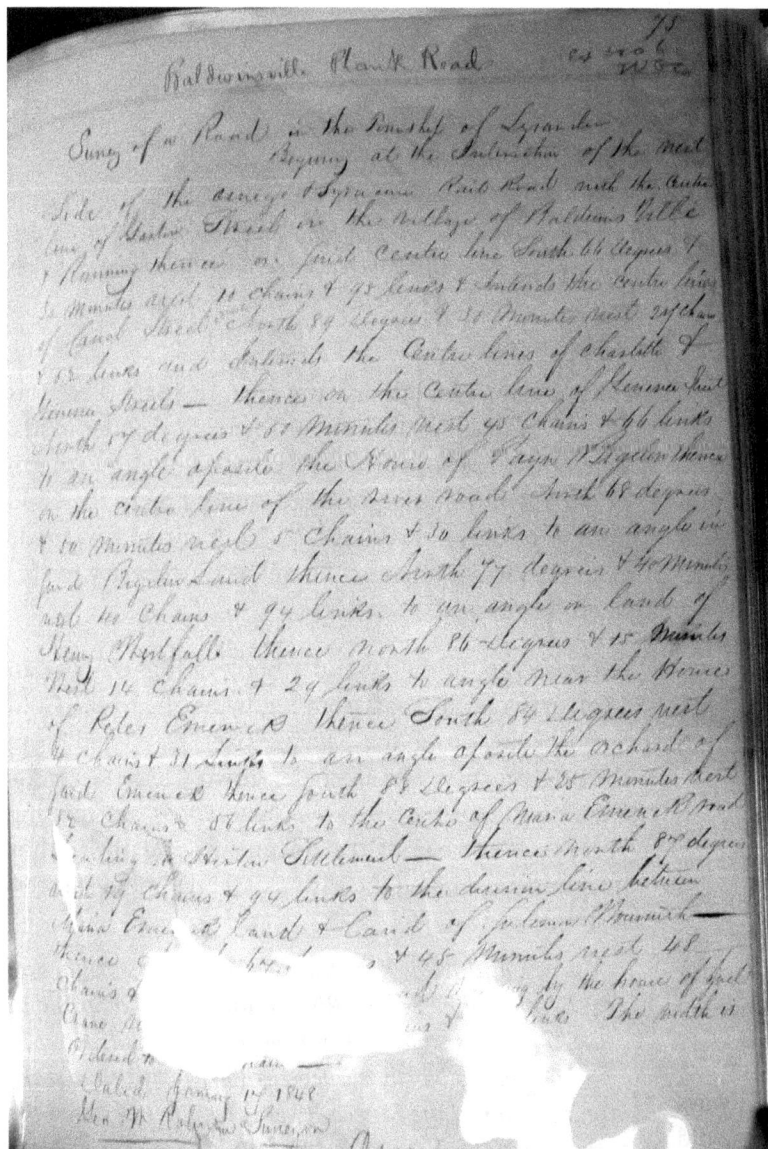

A copy of the survey for the 1848 Baldwinsville Plank Road extending from the Oswego & Syracuse Railroad tracks (Approximately 75 E. Genesee St.) westward through the center of Baldwinsville to the present day Emerick Road, a distance of a little over three miles.

Circa 1920 road construction. Man and beast powered road construction for hundreds of years and into the 1900s. Until the time of mechanization land owners supplied the labor for road maintenance as part of their taxes.

Commissioner of Highways stated:

"I Asher R. Gates Com'r of Highways of the Town of Lysander do determine and agree that there shall be added to District No. 12 all of road district formerly described as District No. 38 of said Town of Lysander and the two districts shall be known as District No. 12. Dated April 2nd 1894. A. R. Gates Com'r of Highways."

Also on the same page the following is entered:

"I Asher R. Gates Commissioner of Highways of the Town of Lysander do determine and agree that the property of Patrick Hurley shall be sett off from District No 77 and added to District No 54, to which District No 54 shall be added from Michael Donahue's corner South to the North line of Dewitt Toll's farm and District No 77 shall hereafter run from Donahue Corner North to the Lamsons and Phoenix Road. Dated at Baldwinsville April 2, 1894. A.R. Gates Commissioner of Highways."

In the 1890s more time and money were expended in improving roads. Stone crushers were rented so stones

that farmers removed from their fields could be crushed to provide a more durable road surface. Proposals for new machinery including road scrapers, stone crushers, rollers and steam engines were often defeated but eventually came into use. Road Commissioners became full-time rather than part time with the increased responsibilities of providing better roads. In 1902, Lysander resolved to spend up to $6,000 on roads, exclusive of bridges. For example, $800 was authorized for a crushed stone surface for one-third-mile on Lamson Road. In 1909, Lysander ordered 20 carloads of crushed stone from the Onondaga County Penitentiary at Jamesville. (Quite likely inmates at the Penitentiary provided the labor to crush and load the stone.)

When new utility services came to the towns, the Road Commissioners' duties increased because of requests to run gas pipe lines, telegraph lines and electric lines over bridges. In 1900, when the new bridge over the Seneca River in Baldwinsville was constructed, the Syracuse, Lakeside and Baldwinsville Railroad was being constructed and permission was given by both Van

A 1915 image of county road construction at Warners. The roadbed was graded and stones from a stone crusher were added to form the base of the road before concrete was poured on top of the stones. Farmers drew the stones with horses and wagon from stone piles that had accumulated on their farms for many years. Photo courtesy of the OHA Museum & Research Center.

Buren and Lysander for the railroad to lay and maintain tracks on the bridge, subject to each town receiving a total of $2,200 over several years.

In 1909, a letter arrived at Lysander from the New York State Department of Highways stating that the Town was not providing the Lysander Highway Superintendent enough money to do his best or most economical work on the roads. It further stated that if the Town were to increase the amount it spent on roads from $2,761 to $6,000 the State would increase its state aid from $1,381 to a maximum of $3,000.

It was amusing to note that in 1912 Lysander rented a car for $12 to carry the Town Board on a highway inspection tour. It may have been the first time some of the Board had ever ridden in an automobile. In previous years their inspection tours were with horse and buggy.

In 1913, when Onondaga County helped improve Lamson Road, a water pump in the middle of the Little Utica four-corners had to be moved. The well underneath the pump was capped below the highway and a water pipe run to private property nearby. The purchase price for the land where the pump was located was $1 and a deed was granted to the Town of Lysander. As a result, horses passing through Little Utica could continue to enjoy a drink of water!

Ralph Bratt, who was born in 1917 and lived on Tater Road, told the author that in 1926 the Town of Lysander was the first town in the area to plow roads with mechanized equipment. This is partially verified by a resolution in the December 31, 1925 Lysander Town minutes authorizing the purchase of one Frick snow plow for $725.

As the 20th century progressed, a rapid increase in the number of trucks and cars brought major improvements to our highways. In 1914, improvements to the Baldwinsville-Cold Springs Road (Route 370) cost $54,157. The State paid half of the cost with Onondaga County paying $18,954 and Lysander $8,123. By 1929, Lysander had 121 miles of roads: 39.6 miles of town improved roads, 35.25 unimproved town roads, 33.26 miles of county roads and 12.84 miles of county highways. (No criteria is given as to the difference between county roads and county highways but the author is suspicious that highways were improved more than roads.)

After 1912, significant improvements began to take place on major local and state highways. A *Post Standard* article, cited in the February 15,1912 *Gazette & Farmers' Journal*, notes that contracts were going to be let for nearly 27 miles of State highways in Onondaga County. Included were 5.61 miles for the Euclid-Baldwinsville Road (currently Route 31).

Route 370 between Baldwinsville and Plainville became a concrete highway in about 1919. An article in the March 6,1919 *Gazette & Farmers' Journal* stated that Baldwinsville had borrowed $15,000 the previous year to pay the expense of paving the village portion of West Genesee St. beyond the 16 feet in the center paved by the state, an additional width of nine feet on the Downer St. part of the Baldwinsville-Jordan Road and additional paving on two areas of the north-south road through the village. This work was anticipated to be started in 1919.

At the time these and other area roads were improved from gravel to a concrete road surface, there was a great deal of preparatory work involved in straightening curves and minimizing hills.

The road from Plainville to Jack's Reef became concrete a few years later. The author's father drew stones to a stone crusher located near the west end of Gates Road during the winter of 1923 as a means of earning money. Crushed stone was used both as a base for the highway and mixed with sand, water and Portland cement for the wearing surface. These concrete roads are still in use, although hidden by layers of asphalt that have been applied over the years.

In 1921, Lysander Supervisor L.E. Scriber and Highway Superintendent John Tyler took a party of Baldwinsville businessmen on a road inspection trip. The town had purchased a Keystone steam shovel and was using two dump trucks with it to haul gravel for improving Spragueville Road. Tyler told the party that it had cost the town only thirty-one and three-fourths cents to gravel a running foot of road with this mechanized equipment whereas during the previous year, shoveling the gravel on dump-wagons by hand and hauling it

A photograph of a steam engine powering a rock crusher circa 1920. The farmer with horses and wagon is bring large stones from his farm for crushing to make a base and topping for improving roads. This was a common sight around Onondaga County between 1890 and 1930 as roads were gradually improved. Photo courtesy of the OHA Museum & Research Center.

with horses, it had cost eighty-two and one-half cents a running foot. Scriber said that the town would be able to reduce highway taxes by at least $1.25 per $1,000 the next year because of the large cost savings.[5]

Many people have never known that there was a Town highway garage in the hamlet of Lysander and those that knew about it probably wondered why. In 1927, the Town of Lysander purchased a warehouse property in the village of Lysander, formerly owned by the Central New York Tobacco Growers' Association Inc. of Lysander, for use as a town highway garage. The buildings cost only $900 and because part of the highway crew lived nearby, the building saved many miles and much time reaching roads that needed plowing or repairing.

Construction of new roads was not as continuous in the 20th century as it had been in the early 19th century but still occurred. In 1928, the Town of Lysander purchased land from several farmers for a new road from Belgium to Cold Springs. A few years later, during the early 1930s, a great deal of road improvements were made under the auspices of the Works Progress Administration

---

5   *Gazette & Farmers' Journal* August 4, 1921

(WPA) and the County Works Administration (CWA). Through these programs, Lysander, in 1933, authorized bonding of $15,000 for Church Road as a means of providing work to help take care of the unemployed. When improving Tater Road about the same time, there were 12 to 15 teams of horses, housed on one of the road's adjacent farms, for work on the road. It is likely that the same methods were used on Church Road and other roads. A priority, during the depression of the 1930s, was to provide work for people rather than to use labor saving mechanized equipment.

Van Buren Roads

The Town of Van Buren was formed from the Town of Camillus by an act of the New York State legislature in 1829. The first Van Buren town meeting was held on April 28, 1829 during which Charles Turner, Henry Cook and David Wiles were named as Highway Commissioners. At that meeting, highway overseers were named for 33 road districts. It is noteworthy that in the Town minutes the overseers were sometimes referred to as road masters and at other times as path masters. Considering that most of the roads in 1829 were very primitive, the term 'path' seems more appropriate than 'road.'

A view looking north in Warners in 1904. The old Methodist church is on the left with the hitching barn to house the worshipers' horses during services.

A photograph of E. Sorrel Hill Road showing the home of John Klotz on the right. In the late 1800s and the early 1900s this scene is typical of most country roads. Photo courtesy of the OHA Museum & Research Center.

In the early 1800s, the Town of Van Buren, as well as Lysander, had only one meeting a year and the minutes of those meetings contain little other than the names of the elected Town officers. In 1830, Van Buren did pass a resolution providing for a fine of $5 for anyone allowing his buck sheep or his boar to run at large on a public highway.

At Van Buren's 1853 meeting, the Town voted that $250 be collected in taxes for use by the Commissioners of Highways and by 1889 the amount of money spent on highways had increased to $692.05. In the 1890s there were also references regarding the construction of iron bridges over Dead Creek and Crooked Brook. In 1899, a resolution was passed authorizing the Commissioner of Highways to have 300 yards of stone crushed for each of two road districts. The 1890s were the beginning of

significant improvement to roads in the Town where heavier traffic required improvements. Farmers were beginning to draw stone from their stone piles and stone fences to a steam powered stone crusher.

In the 1890s, road districts increasingly worked together as larger, more expensive equipment became available for road work. A resolution from a 1892 Van Buren Town meeting stated that a 'road machine' (it was likely an iron grader pulled by horses to level ruts in the road) was purchased by a group of seven road districts. Later that year 'road machine' bills were authorized to be paid for three districts, which had rented one rather than making a purchase. A resolution by the Town in 1904 authorized the expenditure of $200 for a road scraper. Mechanization was gradually arriving.

23

In 1902, the Van Buren Town Board inspected their town roads. After their inspection they directed the path masters of Districts 7, 8 and 10 to work out their tax time on the State Road and authorized the path masters to complete the graveling of that road at town expense. Normally the path masters would obtain gravel or crushed stone that would be charged to the road district but in this case the Town furnished the stone because it was an improvement to a State Road.

A variety of resolutions passed by the Town of Van Buren in the ongoing years reflect the gradual improvement of the roads and the Town's gradually increasing investment in them. In 1907, the commissioner of Highways was authorized to crush 1,000 yards of stone and to buy another 200 yards. A year later the Superintendent received $3 a day and was authorized to hire an engine and a stone crusher, not to exceed $12 a day for up to 100 days. Also, in 1909, there began to be references regarding the removal of snow from public highways when the town appointed 22 road overseers, at the rate of 40 cents an hour, for the purpose of clearing the roads of snow. There was nothing specific stated but a team of horses with sled (bobs) and a small plow attached to the side of the sled was likely the method used by the overseers to remove the snow. Ralph Bratt advised me that this was the method his father used on Tater Road in the Town of Lysander and the author can remember his father using the same method on the roadways on his farm. Only a portion of the snow was removed. It did level the snow and make the roads passable for horse and cutter or sleighs.

A.J. Christopher from his column, *Paving of Cooper Street* in the September 29,1960 issue of *The Baldwinsville Messenger,* relates a variety of interesting facts concerning the construction of Cooper St. (now Maple Rd. and part of Rt. 48 south of Baldwinsville) where his family lived. A four mile portion of this road was first paved in 1912. Previously it had been a dirt road, often with ruts and holes, and with weeds along its sides. The only powered equipment used in its construction was a steamroller with the remainder of the work completed by men and horses. The roadbed was graded, covered with crushed stone and then sprinkled with a coating of tar. The steamroller was used to force the tar and crushed stone together. It was called a macadamized road, experimental at the time, but copied after a technique developed many years before by a Scotsman named MacAdam. In the process of building the road

an old gas line from the days of gas well production in Baldwinsville and a cinder track for bicycles that had followed the road as far as Long Branch were removed. Two temporary buildings were constructed, one for the steam roller operator's family and another to house 15 laborers. Crushed stone and barrels of tar were hauled from the nearest freight stations by teams of horses pulling dump wagons. Two portable tar kettles were used to melt the tar and men sprinkled the tar on the crushed stone with sprinkling cans similar to ones used for watering flowers. The road building project lasted several months with the laborers receiving $2 for a nine hour day and the men with teams receiving $4 for the same length of day. The road did not hold up very well and in 1927 numerous curves were removed and the road surface was replaced with concrete. Additional improvements to this road were made in 1937.

Apparently the winter of 1916 was difficult because in March the Van Buren Town Board authorized an emergency loan to highways of $300 for the removal of snow. In 1922, the Town authorized the purchase of snow fence. Snow fence was commonly placed parallel to and about 100 feet from the prevailing wind side of the road. The intent was to stop the snow before it drifted onto the road. Serious snow removal was addressed by the Town in 1938 when they purchased a Walters snow fighter for $10,500. This truck had a four wheel drive, a powerful engine and a reputation as an excellent snow removal machine.

In 1910, VanBuren made other road improvements possible with the purchase of a Buffalo roller for $2,900 and a Climax road hone (a machine similar to what we would call a grader today) for $2,250. Horses pulling a road scraper and man with his rake and shovel were being gradually replaced. In 1935, a load was lifted from both Van Buren and Lysander's road responsibilities when the State of New York assumed responsibility for the bridge over the Seneca River in Baldwinsville.

Bridges, Repairs and Replacement

With the Seneca River dividing the towns of Lysander and Van Buren, coupled with numerous small streams flowing to the river, bridges became essential for land transportation both in and between the two towns. Bridges were especially important in Lysander, which was separated from four other towns by the river along more than 20 miles of shoreline. Once a bridge was constructed it had to be maintained and periodically replaced.

Temporary Bridge Carries Baldwinsville Traffic

OPEN TO TRAFFIC. Temporary bridge over Seneca River at Baldwinsville has been opened to traffic pending the completion of new span 252 feet long.

A 1937 photograph of the temporary bridge across the Seneca River in Baldwinsville that was used while the old one was replaced. The new bridge (the present bridge) was opened November 1, 1937. Planks were placed lengthwise the length of the bridge for vehicles to drive upon. Spaces were left between the rows of plank making driving across the bridge a challenge for timid drivers. The author can still remember the rumble of the planks while riding across the bridge.

Repairing and replacing bridges was a constant challenge and increasingly more costly as the years progressed. Wood structures evolved into iron and, except for small bridges over creeks, work needed to be contracted with bridge building companies. In Lysander, both repairs and new bridge construction over the Seneca River required joint projects with Elbridge at Jack's Reef, Van Buren in Baldwinsville, Salina at Cold Springs and Schroeppel for the Oswego River at Phoenix. Each of these bridges was large and very costly to build and repair.

The cost of building new bridges is shown vividly in the town records. Records show C.T. Connor being paid $25

for a new bridge near Baird's Corners (near Lysander hamlet) and S. Fancher receiving $50 for building a new bridge in Baldwinsville. In 1847, A.B. Maynard was paid $50.63 for building a bridge over Ox Creek and in 1852 Sam Avery received $150 for his contract in building a new bridge at Pheonix. It is likely that an equal amount was paid by the Town of Schroeppel in Oswego County.

The earliest practical way to cross the Seneca River at Cold Springs was on Drake's Ferry until an act of the legislature in 1823 stipulated that a free bridge was to be constructed that would not impair navigation. Before many years this bridge was replaced, and in 1870 it was

This is a photograph of the covered bridge crossing the Seneca River at Jack's Reef. The bridge, constructed in 1838 or 1839, was 282 feet long and made entirely of wood. It had a long life as it was not replaced until 1923 when the road between Plainville and Jack's Reef was improved from gravel to concrete. Photo courtesy of the OHA Museum & Research Center.

again replaced. The bridge was also replaced in 1905 followed by another replacement in the 1960s.[6]

An article in the October 6,1904 *Gazette & Farmer' Journal* indicates that the existing Cold Springs Bridge of 1904 was condemned and that the State would immediately establish a ferry and a new bridge would be constructed costing $15,000 to $20,000, with the State paying half and the towns of Salina and Lysander each one quarter. There is an interesting side note regarding borrowing to pay for the bridge. When Lysander borrowed $5,000 for its share of repairs from the State Bank in Baldwinsville, the bank specified that the money be repaid in gold coin!

A bridge of considerable note was built at Jack's Reef in 1838 or 1839. It was a covered bridge, 282 feet long and constructed entirely of wood. The bridge served its purpose until 1923 when it was replaced by a concrete bridge. The main frame of the bridge was of hand-hewn timbers cut from a nearby woods. An occasional

steamboat found it necessary to remove its smokestack to pass under the bridge.[7] The author has heard stories from his father and other farm neighbors telling of carrying snow to lay on the floor inside the covered bridge so that horses could pull loaded sleds over the bridge.

As wagon loads increased in size and motor vehicles began to come into use, the safety of the bridges became an issue. In 1904, the Town of Lysander passed a resolution stating there would be a penalty of $5 for any person driving faster than a walk on the bridges over the Seneca River and the Oswego River at Phoenix.

Over the years there were numerous resolutions concerning repairs to the bridge over the Seneca River in Baldwinsville. In 1899, an engineer hired by the Towns declared the Seneca River bridge unsafe and was instructed by the Towns of Lysander and Van Buren to submit plans and estimated cost for a new bridge. The engineer was also instructed to determine what it might cost to repair the present bridge. It was decided

6   Christopher, A.J. *Several Bridges Have Stood at Cold Spring, The Baldwinsville Messenger* June 25, 1970

7   Christopher, A.J. *More on Bridges at Jack's Reef, The Baldwinsville Messenger* July 1, 1965

to construct a new bridge because repairs might be of short duration and unseen weaknesses could appear.

There were numerous joint meetings of the Lysander and Van Buren Town Boards in the process of obtaining a new bridge. A contractor from East Berlin, CT submitted the lowest bid of eight received, varying in cost from $36,499 to $42,000 exclusive of masonry and bridge surface. Bonds were authorized by both Town Boards at 3 1/2% interest, with a $1,000 bond to be paid each year by each town. Brick and tile for the bridge surface came from Ohio. Upon completion, the bridge was 255 feet long and 48 1/2 feet wide. On June 18, 1900, less than a year after the old bridge had been declared unsafe, the new bridge was completed and the officials of both towns were so pleased they passed resolutions expressing their pleasure with the results. The new bridge was an example of fine cooperation between the two towns.

The 1900 bridge was the fourth bridge over the Seneca River in Baldwinsville. The first, in 1809, was a toll bridge constructed by Dr. Jonas Baldwin and was discussed earlier. The succeeding bridges, paid for with public money, were toll-free. In 1837, the second, also authorized by the legislature, was a covered bridge costing approximately $3,000 with $1,500 from Onondaga County, $800 from Lysander and $650 from Van Buren. In 1865, the third bridge was completed at a cost of $9,627.50 and paid for by the two towns. The fourth bridge, constructed in 1900, described in the previous paragraph, cost between $40,000 and $50,000, split evenly between the two towns. (The exact total cost is not recorded because of more than one contract.) The fifth bridge, which opened on November 1, 1937, was paid for by the State and cost $129,590.90.[8]

8   Christopher, A.J. *State Built Present Village Bridges, The Baldwinsville Messenger* January 10, 1973

A picture of the demolition of the third Baldwinsville bridge crossing the Seneca River in 1899.

As bridges across the rivers in the Town of Lysander gradually needed to be replaced, partial funding began to come from the counties involved and even New York State. In 1911, the bridge crossing the Oswego River and Barge Canal at Phoenix, was replaced at a cost of $100,000. Lysander and Schroeppel each paid $25,000, Onondaga and Oswego Counties together paid a total of $25,000 and New York State paid the remaining $25,000.

No attempt has been made to count the local bridges but there are many and often they are not visible to someone cruising across them in an automobile traveling at 50 miles an hour. Bridges have been a critical component in our ability to travel on roads and have continually been upgraded as their use has increased. Roads and bridges will always be an important segment in transportation.

Roads, of course, are made to be used. In the next several chapters the various types of uses will be considered, beginning with travel on foot.

CHAPTER 4

Travel on Foot

Sometimes by choice but more often by necessity, a person travels by foot. Without domesticated animals, other than the dog, walking and running were the only means of land transportation for the Native Americans. Running was an accepted part of their lives. Messages from one village or one tribe to another were delivered by runners. The fastest runners were held in esteem. Their ability to run is demonstrated by early mail delivery in Baldwinsville. Before 1807, mail to the few residents at McHarrie's Rifts (later Columbia, still later Baldwin's Bridge and finally Baldwinsville) arrived haphazardly. It first came to Three Rivers or Onondaga Hill, and then on to Columbia carried by some itinerant traveler who then deposited it in a hollow tree, east of the settlement at McHarrie's Rifts until the addressee happened by. In 1807, Oundiaga, an Onondaga Indian chief, became a mail runner. Twice a week, rain, shine or snow, he left Onondaga Hill with the mail at 4:00 a.m., running 40 miles to Oswego in 10 hours. He spent the night in Oswego making the return run with the mail on the following day. According to old records he was never late or failed in his responsibility.[1] Later, probably when the road was improved in 1814, Walter Herrick, the proprietor of the American Hotel in Baldwinsville, ran stages to Syracuse carrying passengers, baggage and mail.[2]

In the late 1700s, before there were any roads, white settlers often came to Central New York, at least part of the way, on foot. If they were traveling on water, once they came to the end of the waterway there was no other choice. Anyone coming to settle and bringing livestock had to drive or lead their animals through the forests. There are numerous references of farm families coming west along the Mohawk to central and western New York, driving and leading their livestock. Often the parents and younger children came ahead while the older children came later bringing the slower moving livestock.

After roads were cut through the forests and continuing into the early 1900s, drovers herded cattle, sheep, geese and turkeys on the highways, taking them to market in the cities. There was no other practical way to move farm livestock to market other than by driving them on the roads. Railroads were not an option for small farms selling a cow, a few sheep, a few turkeys or geese until a large number were accumulated near a railhead. Many taverns catered to the drovers by furnishing yards to hold the animals overnight, and selling feed to drovers that did not bring a sufficient supply with them. As the drovers traveled to markets, farmers along the way often sold livestock to them, and the herd sizes got larger as they neared the market. Most areas of Lysander and Van Buren are sufficiently close to Syracuse to be able to drive livestock to market in one day. Undoubtedly, many times, drovers coming from further west, came through the streets of Baldwinsville as they headed toward Syracuse markets. There was a drover's tavern on Rt. 20, twelve miles east of Syracuse and another on current Rt. 92, five miles east of Syracuse. There was also a hamlet two miles south of Delphi Falls called Gooseville Corners that received its name from the geese being driven to market through the crossroads.

The following quote, from a December 2,1897 article in the *Utica Daily Press,* entitled 'The Old Seneca Turnpike' provides an insight into the extent of the drovers' business.

> *"One of the greatest sources of revenue this road had was from the livestock that passed over it by the thousands. Horses, cattle, sheep, hogs and even turkeys were driven over it, the toll being so much per head. Sometimes a drove of 500 head of cattle would pass over this road and it was singular how such a body of cattle were managed. On account of the danger of stampede,*

1 Palmer, Pearl *Historical Review of the Town of Lysander*, Part 45

2 Christopher, A. J. *First State Road in Region, The Baldwinsville Messenger* June 10, 1971

An image of drovers driving a flock of turkeys from the countryside to be marketed in a metropolitan area. Drovers used the roads to also drive cattle, sheep and geese to market.

caused by a few who were nervous, the cattle were divided into blocks of 100 each and separated about a mile apart. An intelligent steer was picked out to head each block, a bell being tied on him. The steer seemed to understand his business and kept in the middle of the road, all of the rest following him."

Along the early roads it was common to find people walking, usually in a westerly direction, perhaps only a few miles or sometimes more than 100 miles, following the dream of a home, work and prosperity in the lands opening throughout upstate New York. Sometimes they were walking alongside an ox cart or an ox sleigh loaded with their worldly possessions, and other times they were walking with everything they owned on their backs. Numerous residents of the Baldwinsville area had ancestors that came in this manner. The author's great-great grandfather came with his family to Lysander from north of Albany by ox sleigh in the 1820s. Although stagecoaches were operating on the major roadways by the late 1790s, few settlers could afford this luxury.

Many settlers, often new immigrants, walked on our roadways long after the Erie Canal and railroads came into general use because they couldn't afford to ride. Today, we occasionally see hikers walking along the roads for enjoyment but the author remembers quite a few people, usually men and often referred to as tramps, moving from place to place with all of their belongings on their backs during the 1930s. Walking will always be the first choice of travel for very short distances but for the majority of people the distances walked have been gradually decreasing since the area was first settled.

As quickly as paths were cut through the forest, walking became less of an option for people traveling more than short distances. Like roads, which were designed to follow paths of least resistance, people desire to travel from one location to another with limited effort. As paths became roads and as roads improved, man used oxcarts, sleds, wagons and carriages, as discussed in the next chapter, rather than walking.

CHAPTER 5

Travel with Carts, Sleds, Wagons, Sleighs and Carriages

Before 1800 and for some years afterward, other than the occasional lone traveler on horseback and often on foot, settlers coming to Central New York on land traveled by ox or ox team. Winter was the preferable time for settlers to travel because the frozen ground was covered with snow, making it relatively easy for an ox to pull a sleigh piled high with settlers' belongings. During winter there were few ruts in the roads whereas during spring, summer and fall sleds were harder to pull and ox carts often got mired where roads passed through low, swampy areas. In addition, settlers preferred to reach their destination in the late winter to plant seeds in the spring to provide food for the following winter.

In the 1700s and early 1800s, oxen were more common than horses for several reasons. They could be maneuvered around trees and stumps more easily than the faster horse, which was often nervous and jumpy. Oxen, being ruminants, could live off the land eating small bushes, branches and whatever could be found in the forest. Feed for horses needed to be transported along with the settlers' goods unless hay and oats could be purchased en route, which was not possible in unsettled areas. Oxen, castrated bull calves from cows, were substantially less expensive than horses. Near the end of the ox's useful life it could be slaughtered as food for the family. Each of these factors contributed to make oxen more common than horses for our early settlers. According to records, several hundred sleighs (low and flat with wide wooden runners) heading west crossed the Hudson River in a single day in February, 1795.[1]

In 1792, Baldwinsville's first settlers, the McHarries, came from Maryland following the trail made by General Sullivan along the Susquehanna in 1779, and continuing north to the Seneca River above the Finger Lakes. Since they floated down the Seneca to what is now Baldwinsville on a watercraft, they must have found a settler further west to trade with or may have constructed a raft from the trees in the forest. An example of an extended family with means coming to the area occurred in 1815 when the Rulef Schenck family traveled 120 miles from Montgomery County to Plainville with five loaded wagons.[2]

As roads improved and Central New York's population increased, the number of oxen decreased, and horses more commonly provided the power to transport people over the roadways. There are no New York census numbers for oxen until 1845 when 2,454 oxen were recorded in Onondaga County, decreasing to 683 only 10 years later. There is no question that there were more oxen in the early 1800s than in 1845, when the lands were well settled and the roads were substantially improved. By 1845, there were 16,968 horses in Onondaga County compared with 9,871 in 1825.

During the last half of the 1800s, the horse became as essential to every family that could afford one, as the automobile is to families today. Wealthier families often had a horse and carriage for both father and mother, and sometimes a fine carriage pulled by a matched team. Carriages were used during the spring, summer and fall with sleighs their replacement when snow was on the ground. Homes, whose owners had horses, usually had a carriage house in the rear to house the horses, carriages and sleighs. It was normally a two story building with the upper level used to store hay and straw for bedding. The harness, blankets for the horses, robes for the passengers and oats for the horses were stored on the lower level. A pile of fine organic fertilizer gradually accumulated outside the back door of the carriage house as winter progressed and was spread in the spring to fertilize next summer's garden.

Horses also furnished the power to pull the wagons and sleighs that transported raw materials, finished products

---

1 Christopher, A.J. *Oxen Brought Early Pioneers, The Baldwinsville Messenger* June 24, 1971

2 Christopher, A.J. *Oxen Brought Early Pioneers, The Baldwinsville Messenger* June 24, 1971

A Currier & Ives print of an oxcart pulled by a yoke of oxen. Many Central New York settlers came to this area with their worldly possessions piled on either a sled or a cart pulled by oxen.

A photograph taken at Williamsburg, VA of a family hauling wood in their oxcart. Oxen were inexpensive, compared to horses, and because they are ruminants could obtain their food from the plants in the forests, whereas horses needed grass or hay.

A typical winter scene in Baldwinsville between 1820 and 1920. Heavy coats, buffalo robes and foot warmers eased the cold on long rides with horse and cutter.

and innumerable items that trucks haul today. Until the opening of the Erie Canal in 1825, horses hauled wheat and other farm products from Buffalo to Albany and brought essentials needed by young communities from Albany to all points west. They transported produce from the farms to the canals and railroads. Horses hauled materials from the canal boats and the railroads to the factories and stores as well as hauling finished goods from stores and factories to the canal boats and the railroad cars. Local merchants provided hitching posts in front of their stores for the convenience of customers coming via horse drawn conveyances.

The vehicles pulled by oxen on the roadways were limited to low flat sleds and ox carts. Before roads were cut through the forest, horses carried only a rider. As roads and bridges came into existence, the variety, size and quantity of horse drawn vehicles increased. Almost everything that was moved, other than on the waterways, was moved by horses and oxen: people, farm produce, business merchandise, industrial raw materials and finished products. A variety of wagons, carriages, sleds and sleighs filled the needs of villagers,

farmers, business and industry throughout Central New York from the late 1700s into the first part of the 1900s, changing gradually as advancements were made.

When the Baldwinsville area was first being settled, a wagon or a carriage was nowhere to be seen. Without roads there was no convenient way for them to reach this area and no place for them to be used. Sleds were used 12 months of the year and could be made by almost anyone by splitting part of a tree trunk into slabs and placing these slabs on the Y crotch of a tree. As the community developed, roads were cut through the forests and wagons began to appear. There is no record of when the first wagon shop came to Baldwinsville but Edith Hall in her book, *History of Baldwinsville,* stated that there were four carriage shops in 1849. The *1855 New York Census* noted that there were six coach and wagon shops in Lysander and one spoke shop in Van Buren. (Historically, shops described as coach, wagon and carriage made any one of the three and sometimes all three in addition to sleighs.) By 1859, there were wagon and carriage shops in Lysander, Plainville, Jacksonville, Van Buren, Baldwinsville and, undoubtedly, there were others scattered around Lysander and Van Buren. If there was a wheelwright available to make wheels, almost any blacksmith could produce wagons. Wagons and carriages were as important to the people of the 1800s and the early 1900s as automobiles and trucks are to us today.

Farmers first used sleds to move produce from the fields to the barn and to market during all seasons of the year. When a wagon shop came to the area, the farmer bought a wagon as soon as he could afford one. A much larger load could be hauled from the fields or to market when there was no snow on the ground. The family could also climb onto the wagon to go to the neighboring village without the need to spend money for a carriage. The democrat wagon (not a political name but referring to the fact that moderate income families owned them) was a light weight wagon that could be fitted with removable seats permitting the wagon to be used for either passengers or merchandise.

The term carriage is quite confusing as both wagons and carriages need wheels with a carriage to attach the wheels. They both also need a body, although with a wagon it may be just a few boards. Even though a wagon is a carriage for a great variety of items including people, common terminology refers to vehicles that only carried people as carriages. Each manufacturer of carriages and wagons had his own techniques and slight differences. As one manufacturer came up with improvements others copied them, similarly to the changes in automobiles today. There were a number of specific types as there are different types of motor vehicles today: freight wagons both light and heavy, carriages that were plain and fancy, carriages for speed and those made to carry larger numbers of people. Some were adapted for a special purpose: delivery of ice, milk or groceries. If a customer had a special need the wagon and carriage manufacturers met that need to the best of their ability. It was a period of production of one item at a time custom designed to satisfy the buyer.

Roads were not plowed in the winter until the 1920s. Whenever the snow accumulated, the wagons and carriages were stored in the barn until spring. Cutters for carrying passengers in the snow were originally almost

A variety of horse pulled buggies at the Baldwinsville four-corners on October 12, 1887, the day of the dedication of the Civil War Monument which now rests in Riverview Cemetery.

A photo of A.M. Hudson delivering milk with horse and wagon. Housewives brought containers out to Mr. Hudson and he dipped whatever amount was desired from his milk can.

Previous to the days of electricity and refrigeration, the iceman's wagon was an important service for the community. This photograph is of two ice delivery wagons of E.E. Ellsworth located on Crooked Brook on Ellsworth Road in the Town of Van Buren.

A picture of a farmer on W. Genesee St. delivering a load of tobacco leaves, pressed into bundles, to a tobacco warehouse in Baldwinsville. The Methodist Church is in the background on the left. Notice the dirt street and the raised board sidewalk.

A man delivering flour to customers' homes in Baldwinsville around 1900. Most families had no means of carrying their purchases other than in their arms so groceries and heavy items like flour were delivered directly to the homes.

entirely made of wood with wooden runners and only a piece of metal on the bottom. In the latter part of the 1800s, the entire runner was made of iron and the body had metal reinforcement. Cutters became much lighter and if they tipped over could be turned upright by one person. Some were open and some had a canopy to help keep some of the snow off of the passengers.

Travel by cutters or bobs in the winter required special protection for both horses and travelers. Even though it may have been cold and stormy, horses worked up a sweat. Special blankets were carried to put on the horses when they reached their destination. Buffalo robes or heavy blankets were used to cover the legs and laps of passengers and drivers. Hoods and ear coverings were commonly used and heated soapstones were placed under the riders' feet. Sometimes a small soapstone was held in a passenger's hands. Often some coals from the fireplace were put in a special container and placed under the robe to help provide warmth for the passengers' legs and feet.

Farmers and some of the business and manufacturing enterprises used what is called 'bobs' to replace their wagons in the winter. Bobs were similar to a wagon although in place of wheels there were four runners. They were pulled by a team of horses and were excellent in the snow. Packed snow developed on most of the roads, gradually building in height as the winter progressed. Sometimes where the road passed through a low area or where a row of trees caused the snow to drift, the cutters and bobs left the roadway to travel in the adjoining field. On other occasions farmers sometimes fastened a homemade wooden plow to the side of the bobs to help make the road more passable. The author remembers riding on bobs many times hauling wood, livestock waste to the fields, and even being transported to the Plainville school, along with a number of fellow students, on a blustery winter day. One of the things the driver had to contend with, especially when it warmed up on a winter day, was the accumulation of hard packed snow on the bottom of the horses' feet. It was very uncomfortable for the horse so the driver carried

A heavy wagon for transporting big loads (referred to as trucks before what we now consider trucks came into existence) near the corner of Water and Canton Streets circa 1900. Notice the tracks for the spur of the Syracuse & Baldwinsville Railroad in the street. The Lester Meroney horseshoeing and repair shop is in back of the wagon and has a sign offering Walter Wood farm equipment for sale.

a snow pick and periodically stopped to remove the accumulation of snow and ice on the bottom of the horses' feet.

With the introduction of the automobile many carriage manufacturers had no choice but to close shop because of lack of sales. In the Syracuse area, Harvey Moyer had a large business producing carriages and made the move to manufacturing automobiles. He, like many others throughout the United States, was not successful and went out of business in six years. Wagons continued to be produced because of their need on the many farms in the area. The number of wagon manufacturers decreased though, because of their manufacture by large centralized agricultural corporations. The Haywood Wagon Company was at 34 East Genesee St. from 1903 until 1914 when it moved to Newark, New York. Haywood made contractors' dump wagons, the predecessor of today's dump trucks, asphalt, garbage and coal wagons and stone spreaders.

Almost all the functions provided by automobiles and trucks today were once provided by horse and wagon. In this old photo we have the dog catcher wagon with a dog who appears that it might be in charge!

Many individuals and families owned carriages and cutters as well as the horses to pull them. When travel was necessary for people who didn't have these conveniences or if longer distance travel was required, the stagecoach became an important means of travel.

A beautifully matched team of carriage horses on W. Genesee St. in Baldwinsville in front of where the village hall now stands. Men took great pride in a fine team of well trained horses. Notice how well they are standing and holding their heads high.

An image of a team of matched horses pulling a delivery wagon from The Great Atlantic & Pacific Tea Company (A&P) at 78 Salina St. in Syracuse around 1900. There was an A&P store in Baldwinsville on the north side of W. Genesee St. in Baldwinsville for many years during the mid 1900s. Notice the cobblestone curb along the street. Courtesy of the OHA Museum & Research Center.

A horse drawn hearse is entering Riverview Cemetery in Baldwinsville.

A photograph of Sophie Voorhees, one of the granddaughters of Colonel James Voorhees, with her horse and democrat wagon at the Syracuse, Lakeside & Baldwinsville Stop 89. A democrat wagon had no political connection but was a lightweight wagon with removable seats that could be also used to carry merchandise.

The Vanderbilts arriving at the New York State Fair in a fancy carriage. Commodore Vanderbilt was the principle owner of the New York Central Railroad and came to the fair with horses and carriages on a special train in his own well appointed railroad car.

The current home of Sally Dayger on W. Genesee St. and its nearby carriage house in Baldwinsville. For many years it was the home and office of Dr. George Hawley. In Dr. Hawley's early years of practicing medicine he kept a buggy and horse in the carriage house to facilitate his travel to the homes of sick patients scattered around the Baldwinsville countryside.

Imagine an ambulance, pulled by a team of galloping horses, with a seriously injured person inside, heading to the nearest hospital! This was the situation in large cities during the late 1800s. More often, however, there wasn't a hospital available and if there was one in the city, the injured person would have been loaded on the back of the nearest wagon.

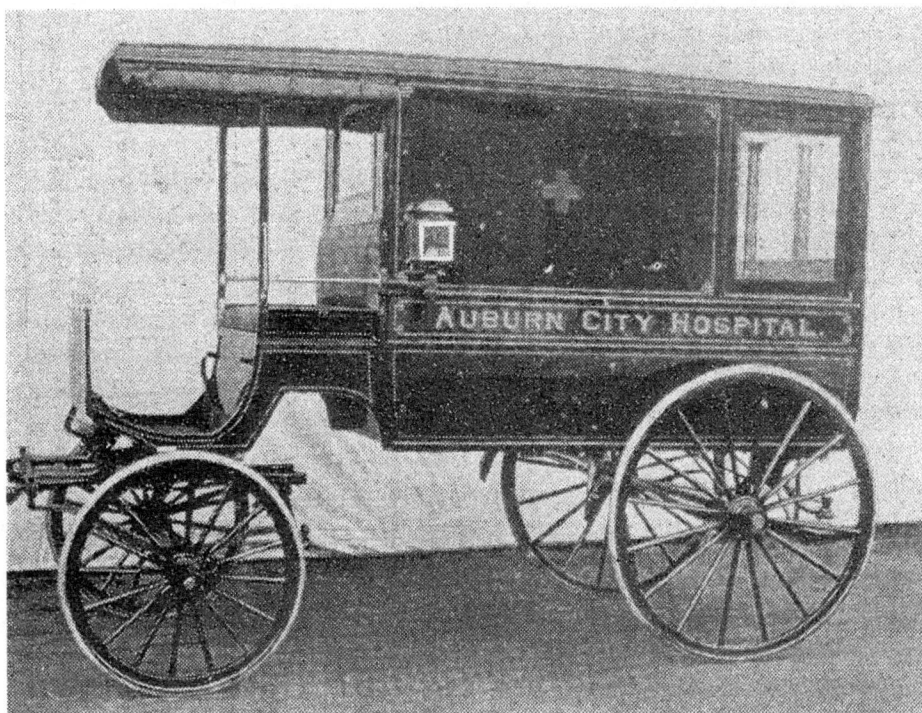

A photograph of Mailman Grant Adsit performing the Rural Free Delivery service in the Baldwinsville area.

A photo of US Mail delivery with horse and cutter. Regardless of the weather the mail got through! Often when the roads were filled with snow travel was across the farmers' fields. Courtesy of the OHA Museum & Research Center.

Watering troughs for horses were essential wherever horses traveled during both summer and winter. The watering trough shown was in downtown Syracuse. One still exists, without the water, at the four corners in the hamlet of Lysander. Courtesy of the OHA Museum & Research Center.

Even ice cream was hauled to retail stores by horse and wagon around 1900. Notice the paved street and what appears to be a concrete curb. The vertical lines on the horse come from rawhide fly strips that move up and down and back and forth as the horse moves along the streets. Flies were a serious problem in cities and villages during warm weather because of the tons of organic fertilizer produced daily by horses and other livestock. Courtesy of the OHA Museum & Research Center.

CHAPTER 6

Stagecoaches

Most of us have seen stagecoaches in movies of the West, with galloping horses, driver sitting high on the coach holding tightly to the reins, dust flying and town's people eagerly anticipating the arrival of passengers. It is hard to imagine but similar scenes occurred throughout our Central New York area, including Baldwinsville, in the 1800s.

Stagecoaches, pulled by horses, carried mail and passengers in New York from the late 1600s until into the early 1900s. Initially there were stagecoaches only in the populated areas along the Hudson River corridor, before most of New York had been settled. After the Revolutionary War, as the population spread, stagecoaches became numerous wherever a need for them occurred that could be profitably filled. Other than boat, the stagecoach was the only method of public transportation until canals and railroads arrived. One of the first active stagecoach runs in Upstate New York was between Albany and Schenectady because rapids prohibited travel on that stretch of the Mohawk River.

At Schenectady travelers could go west on the Mohawk River and at Albany go south on the Hudson River. Once there were roads, stage routes were extended as shown in the following notice printed in the May 27,1793 *Albany Gazette*, courtesy of Richard Palmer.

Albany Gazette
May 27, 1793

Western Stage. - The Subscriber has erected a stage, which will commence running the tenth of May next weekly, from the city of Albany thro' Schenectady to Johnstown and Canojohary the next day. The stage will leave every Friday morning at 6 o'clock and arrive at Canojohary the next day. Will leave Canojohary on Tuesday morning at the same hour, and arrive in Albany the day following.

This stage being erected for the accommodation of passengers, the fare is fixed at only three pence per mile. Each passenger is allowed 14 lb. baggage gratis & 150 lb.

A stagecoach on W. Genesee St. in Baldwinsville during the late 1800s. Notice the number of both men and women sitting on top of the stagecoach. When traveling over the rough dirt roads of the day, passengers must have clung to their seats.

baggage is rated equal to a passenger. The Subscriber by endeavoring to merit the patronage of those gentlemen & ladies who may honor him with their company assures himself that he shall gain the approbation and countenance of the public in general - render a communication into the Western Country sure, cheap & expeditious - and eventually benefit himself - The public's devoted servant. MOSES BEAL.

April 29th, 1793.

M.B. He will occasionally go as far as the Little Falls if desired.

A September 3,1825 advertisement in the *New York Spectator,* advertising Powell & Thorp's stagecoach line shows the extent of stagecoach travel by 1825.

"Coaches leave our office at No. 365 North Market Street for the West in the following order. The mail coach travels by day light only - leaving Albany every day at 3:00 o'clock P.M. lodge at Amsterdam, and arrive at Utica next day; at Auburn the second; passing Geneva and Canandiagua, to Avon and Rochester the third; Buffalo and Lewiston the fourth day from Albany. Returns in the same order."

"The Pilot Mail coach leaves Albany every day, at 11 o'clock, P.M. passing Utica, Syracuse (Salt Works) Auburn, Geneva, Canandaigua, and Batavia to Buffalo, through in three days. Returning, leaves Buffalo, at 9 o'clock, P.M. and travels in the same order."

"Cherry Valley, Cooperstown, and Rochester Mail Coach leaves Albany every day for Cherry Valley, Cooperstown, Madison, Cazenovia, Manlius, Syracuse, Weed's Basin, Montezuma, Lyons, Palmyra, and Pittsford to Rochester, through in three days, crossing the canal thirteen times and returns in the same order."

"Two daily lines of Coaches will pass and repass Niagara Falls every day, one on each side of the river, from Lewiston and Buffalo."

"Extra Coaches with relays of horses will be furnished at Albany, Utica, Auburn, Geneva, Canandaigua, Rochester, Buffalo and Lewiston. Baggage at owners risk. Albany June 1, 1825."

(Author's note: Several of the proprietors' names listed at the bottom were Issac Parker & Co. of Utica, I.M. Sherwood of Auburn, and I. Sherwood of Geneva. It

New York Spectator
September 3, 1825

POWELL & THORP'S
GENERAL MAIL COACH OFFICE,
NO. 365 NORTH-MARKET-STREET, ALBANY
Near the Mansion Houses and Post Office.

COACHES leave this Office, for the WEST, in the following order, to wit :—

THE MAIL COACH,
Travels by day light only—leaving Albany every day at 3 o'clock, P. M. lodge at Amsterdam, and arrive at Utica next day ; at Auburn the second ; passing Geneva, and Canandaigua, to Avon and Rochester the third ; Buffalo, and Lewiston the fourth day from Albany. Returns in the same order.

THE PILOT MAIL COACH,
Leaves Albany every day, at 11 o'clock, P. M. passing Utica, Syracuse (Salt Works.) Auburn. Geneva, Canandaigua, and Batavia to Buffalo, through in three days. Returning, leaves Buffalo, at 9 o'clock, P. M. and travels in the same order.

Cherry Valley, Cooperstown, and Rochester
MAIL COACH,
Leaves Albany every day for Cherry Valley, Cooperstown, Madison, Cazenovia, Manlius, Syracuse, Weed's Basin, Montezuma, Lyons, Palmyra, and Pittsford, to Rochester, through in three days, crossing the canal thirteen times, and returns in the same order.

NIAGARA FALLS.
Two daily lines of Coaches will pass and repass the Falls every day, one on each side of the river, from Lewiston and Buffalo.

EXTRA COACHES,
With relays of Horses will be furnished at Albany, Utica, Auburn, Geneva, Canandaigua, Rochester, Buffalo, and Lewiston.
Baggage at the owners risk.
Albany, June 1, 1825.

POWELL & THORP, Albany, ⎫
ISAAC PARKER & CO. Utica, ⎪
I. M. SHERWOOD, Auburn, ⎪
I. SHERWOOD, Geneva, ⎬ Proprietors.
B. D. COE, Canandaigua, ⎪
ORY ADAMS, Rochester, ⎪
SAMUEL BARTON. Lewiston. ⎭

An 1825 newspaper notice of stagecoach travel between Albany and Western New York. At this time stagecoaches provided the travel needs that were later filled by canals and railroads.

An artist's sketch of the arrival of a stagecoach at the inn. Partly for show and partly for speed the stagecoaches often arrived with the sounding of a horn and dust flying from the wheels. Courtesy of Richard Palmer from p. 61 of his book *The "Old Mail Line" Stagecoach Days in Upstate New York*.

is stated that Sherwood had several hundred horses on stage lines in its heyday. The Sherwood Inn at Skaneateles takes its name from I.M. Sherwood and his stagecoaches.)

Lest anyone romanticize stagecoach travel, it would be well to read the following quote taken from pages 35-39 of M.C. Hand's book about Syracuse, *From a Forest to a City*, written in 1889.

"The old four-horse stage coach was a strong and crude contrivance and as uncomfortable a mode of travel as could be imagined, with the perfume of targrease and reeking horses. Steel springs not having been invented, the coach body was suspended upon heavy leather

straps, and a large rack was fastened on the rear and called the "boot," where baggage was stowed away.

The top was decked over and a strong iron railing placed around the outside of the deck to keep packages from falling off. When passengers were plenty and anxious to go, twelve persons were crowded inside, and I have seen nearly as many on the outside at the same time. Five miles an hour, under such circumstances, was astonishing velocity. A journey from Albany to Buffalo in those days, for ladies and gentlemen who were not strong, was undertaken with much reluctance; for seasickness was as common on such journeys as on a voyage across the ocean, as the egg-shaped box suspended on these straps, or belts, had the motion of a rocking chair.

At that time, when the country was comparatively new, many swamps were bridged over by logs being laid close together for the road and filled in between with coarse gravel which was soon partly forced out, and the most intolerable road was the result.

As the stage went thumping and jolting, log in and log out, over this road the motion of the stagecoach resembled the action of the walking-beam of a high pressure engine, and those occupying the rear seat would have to grasp, with both hands, the straps that were provided to hold on with, to prevent from being thrown headlong from their seats. Under such conditions passengers who were not strong, would soon tire out and be compelled to stop at the taverns and rest until another stage was due, sometimes requiring a week to make the trip from Albany to Buffalo."

Stagecoach travel was not inexpensive. An advertisement in the September 12, 1811 *Albany Gazette* quoted the fare from Albany to Utica at $5.50 and $5.00 from Utica to Geneva. This was at a time when the average wage was less than $1.00 a day.

None of the roads in the towns of Lysander and Van Buren were major east-west highways, so stagecoach travel was over shorter distances, either to the final destination or connecting to other stagecoach lines, railroads or boats for a more distant location. In the early 1800s, there were numerous stagecoaches on the Seneca Turnpike, the Genesee Turnpike and other major turnpikes with numerous inns scattered along these turnpikes to accommodate travelers.

There were stagecoaches traveling from Baldwinsville to Syracuse at an early date, according to an article

THE OLD LAMSON-PHOENIX STAGE

The Lamson-Phoenix Stage carried passengers and freight between the village of Phoenix and the railroad depot at Lamson. Courtesy of the OHA Museum & Research Center.

During winter, the Cicero and Syracuse Stage traveled on runners to carry passengers and mail. The driver braved the cold but the passengers were well protected from the elements. Courtesy of the OHA Museum & Research Center.

An artist's sketch of the trials of stagecoach travel during the winter. Unquestionably this scene occurred numerous times when a stage was caught in a surprise blizzard. Illustration through the courtesy of Richard Palmer

in the *1896 Gazette Semi-Centennial* edition stating, "Stagecoaches to Onondaga or Syracuse carried mail prior to a post office in Baldwinsville that was established in 1815 with Jonas C. Baldwin as postmaster." As time progressed and the population increased, stagecoaches came into greater use. In 1831, Walter D. Herrick opened the American Hotel on the corner of Bridge and Canal Streets in Baldwinsville, and managed a line of stagecoaches that ran to Syracuse via Belle Isle. Passengers traveled from Baldwinsville to Syracuse via Hardscrabble and Fairmount and from Baldwinsville to Oswego by stagecoach until train passenger service arrived in 1848. Later, a stage served as a taxi to transport village residents to the railroad station and travelers on the railroad to the several local hotels or to their homes.[1]

There were also a variety of other stage lines in Lysander and Van Buren until replaced by the automobile. One covered a route from Plainville, Lysander, Wright's Corners to Baldwinsville twice a day. Another traveled between Baldwinsville, Belgium, Phoenix and Cicero.

Stagecoaches varied in size and style. For short routes with limited passenger use, a wagon could be modified with plank seats along the sides and a canvass cover over the top. Longer routes, especially those with stretches of rough corduroy, needed a suspension system to help deaden some of the worst bumps. Since most travelers wanted to reach their destinations as quickly as possible, horses ran at a trot and were changed for fresh horses about every 10 miles. The drivers usually had a run that required several changes of horses. Longer runs on the main turnpikes usually had four horses because of the extra weight of more passengers. Shorter runs with lighter loads required only a two-horse team.

One of the last stagecoaches in the US made regular trips between Cicero and Syracuse on the old plank road as late as 1908.[2] For over 50 years it had successfully competed with the trains that provided service to the same area. It offered service that the trains couldn't or wouldn't provide. Packages were delivered to the customers' doors and the stagecoach would stop along its route to pick up or discharge a single passenger. It was the last of

---

1 Christopher, A.J. *Stage Driver Had Many Duties, the Baldwinsville Messenger* May 25, 1967

2 *Syracuse Herald* November 1, 1908

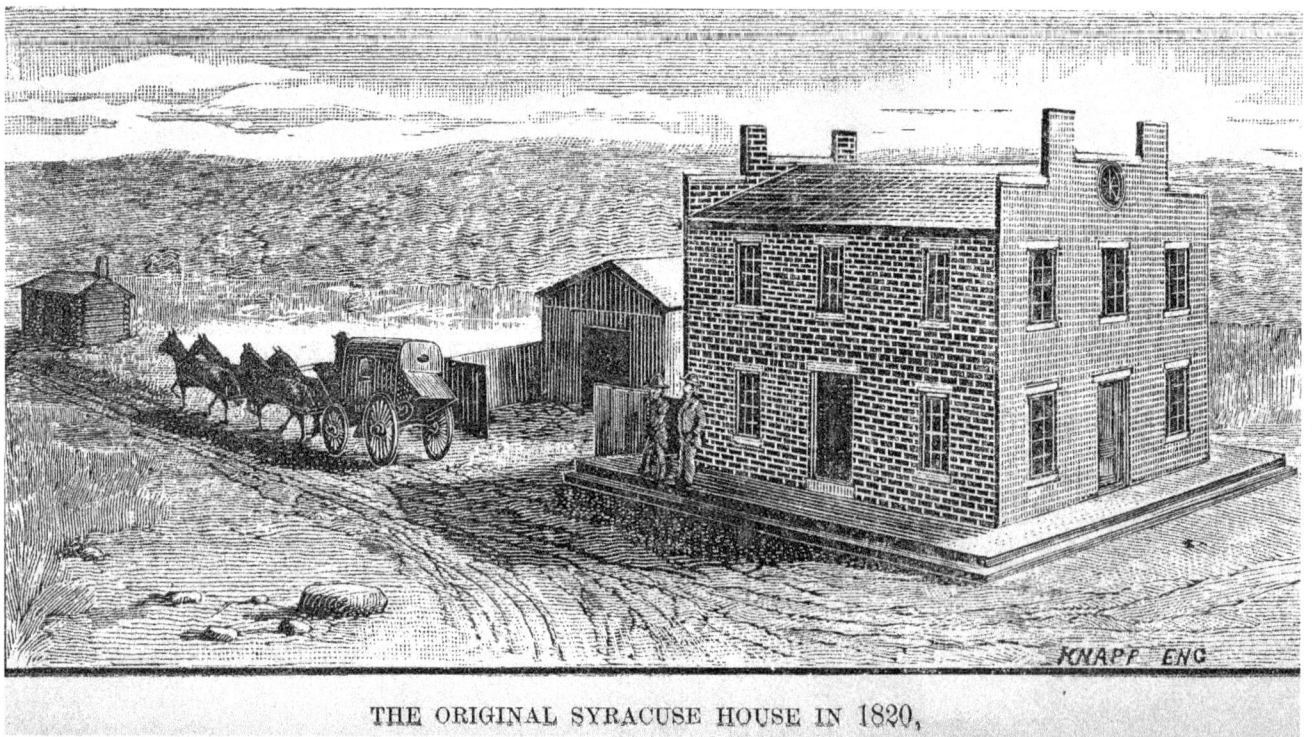

THE ORIGINAL SYRACUSE HOUSE IN 1820,

A sketch of the Old Syracuse House in 1820, which was built to house passengers on stagecoaches traveling through the hamlet of Syracuse. Notice the stagecoach leaving the Inn and the log cabin on the far left. Copied from M.C Hand's book, From a Forest to a City *published in 1889.*

The Cicero-Syracuse stagecoach carried passengers and freight on the old plank road as late as 1908. Even though a railroad traveled the same route, the stagecoach continued successfully after most others had disappeared because of its customer friendly service. Courtesy of the OHA Museum & Research Center.

A stagecoach in front of the old Seneca Hotel in Baldwinsville, located at the northwest corner of Oswego and W. Genesee Streets. Notice the porches on three levels and the large cupola on top of the hotel. It was designed for good natural ventilation during warm weather.

an era that had rapidly vanished with the arrival of the train, trolley, and internal combustion engine powering automobiles, trucks and buses. Stagecoach days remain nostalgic in the minds of many, but after traveling a few miles on the rough roads of the early 1800s, passengers' anticipation of a pleasurable ride disappeared.

There had to be a home for the many horses used by the stagecoach lines. These were the livery stables, as described in the following pages, found in almost every village with a few hundred people.

CHAPTER 7

Livery Stables, Bicycles and Bobsleds

Livery stables provided several needed services in the days of the horse. They were prominent in Baldwinsville until the automobile and truck replaced horses in the 1920s but persisted into the 1930s. People living outside of the village taking the train or trolley to Syracuse left their horse at a livery stable where it was cared for all day and even overnight. Livery stables were somewhat similar to the rental car agencies of today. They kept a few horses, carriages and sleighs that customers could rent for a day or several days. Usually they also sold and traded horses. Ralph Bratt remembers, when he was going to Baldwinsville Academy in 1933, seeing horses from the West coming to Baldwinsville on the train and then being driven up East Genesee Street to the livery stable on the west side of Oswego Street.

'Hitch barn' was another name for a livery stable but usually was considered to offer fewer services and perhaps none other than a crude building to hitch your horse. They were provided in almost all villages as a place for someone from out of the village to leave their horse while conducting business. The owner often brought along a bag of hay for the horse to munch on while waiting for the owner to return. Homer Abbott, who lived three miles east of Baldwinsville on Cold Springs Road, used to leave his horse and cutter at a hitching barn while attending Baldwinsville Academy in 1918. All rural churches and some churches in the village had 'hitch barns' to house the worshipers' horses during Sunday services and other church activities. Hitching barns are still used in Amish communities today.

An advertisement by Driscoll and O'Brien of Canal St. in the 1896 50th Anniversary of *The Gazette & Farmers' Journal*, stated they had a hack, livery, boarding and sale stable. It was operated by Dennis Driscoll and Wm H. O'Brien and offered the 'best rigs' in town for weddings, funerals or parties. Another ad in the same paper by George W. Jones Livery and Boarding Stable offered first

class turnouts. There was also an ad by Chapman & Co., successor to Hiram Betts, noting they were managers of Bus, Mail, Baggage & Express.

Some livery stables had large vehicles, referred to as carryalls or tallyhos, designed to carry as many as 20 passengers for special occasions. The carryalls were designed for use in both the summer and winter. Their large bodies were transferred from wheels to sleigh, running gear in the winter. Normally they were pulled by a team of horses and used for short distances around the village but on longer runs two teams hooked in tandem were used.[1]

A.J. Christopher mentions a number of livery stables in his February 6,1969 article in the *Baldwinsville Messenger* including: DeWitt Toll Co. on Water St. in 1850, Kip Asselstine at 29 Water St., James Holihan also on the South side who had a horseshoeing business, Wormuth Brothers on Canal (E. Genesee), and Driscoll and O'Brien on Canal Street. The local hotels also had livery stables associated with their hotels to harbor their patrons' horses.

Veterinarians were essential in maintaining the health of the many horses in Baldwinsville and surrounding area. Two, Doctors William Long and John Stack who at one time had their offices associated with a livery stable, are remembered by the author because they came to his father's farm in Plainville to treat his cows and horses.

Until the advent of the automobile, public transportation, other than that provided by boat, railroad or trolley, was by a variety of horse drawn conveyances. Almost every small community had at least one carriage or wagon shop. These shops made wagons and carriages to supply the needs of the local population and in some instances

1   Christopher, A.J. *They Rode Carryalls, Tallyhoes, The Baldwinsville Messenger* August 18, 1971

A photograph taken in 1893 of local minister A.B. Davis with his bicycle. This type of bicycle was very difficult to ride, especially on the rough dirt roads of that time. Notice that the rider steers with the smaller wheel and sits on top of the large wheel.

Reverend William Beauchamp, Episcopalian Rector for 35 years and notable local historian, is shown on a relatively modern appearing bicycle circa 1918. Note the street's granite curb and the stone step to assist passengers entering carriages.

became thriving businesses selling their products well beyond the communities' boundaries. One of these, in the early 1900s, was the Haywood Wagon Works mentioned in an earlier chapter.

In the 1800s, renewable energy was the norm and not a buzz word. Farmers grew the hay and grain needed to fuel the oxen and horses of the 19th century. Canal boats were pulled by horses and mules, which used the same renewable fuels. Trains burned wood until later in the century, also a renewable fuel. It wasn't until coal was shipped north from PA to fuel trains and steamboats and the advent of the internal combustion engine powered by newly discovered gasoline, that we moved away from renewable energy. A large portion of the Northern New York economy was based on the production of timothy hay, which was shipped to New York City to fuel its many thousands of horses. When horses were replaced by trucks, automobiles and buses in the 1920s, it badly damaged Northern New York's economy.

Improved roads brought additional services and additional uses for our roadways. Until the early 1900s, when Rural Free Delivery (RFD) originated, rural residents had to pick up their mail at the nearest post office. RFD brought mail directly to a mailbox in front of a rural resident's home erasing much of the isolation experienced previously when they may have picked up their mail at their nearest postoffice once every week or two. In its first years the mail was delivered by horse and buggy until the snows fell, and then by horse and cutter. The daily arrival of the mail and newspaper was eagerly anticipated by most rural families, especially in the days before radios and telephones. RFD was the source of almost all information for rural residents other than any direct contact with neighbors.

In the early 1900s, school districts occasionally began hiring a person to transport children living several miles away from the school. In 1914, District 10, in the Maple Road area, hired a man to transport its children

This circa 1920 image is of two proud sisters and little brother with a bicycle built for two.

This is an 1889 photo of Charles Dow with his tricycle. You will note that there are no tires on the tricycle but just the steel rim to which the spokes are attached.

to school in Baldwinsville. The person employed improvised a small democrat wagon with a covering of white canvas, benches along both sides of the interior and a step on the rear to pick up and carry the 10 or 12 students in the district to school. When winter came the canvas top was transferred to a sleigh for easier travel over the roadways.[2] Until roads were improved and there was motorbus transportation, there were many children that never went to school further than the eighth grade because of the distance to high school. Both of the author's parents boarded at private homes in Baldwinsville while attending high school.

Bicycles

Although bicycles had been in use to a limited extent for 70 years, it wasn't until the 1890s that a bicycle awakening period arrived. The bicycle with the high front wheel nicknamed the 'penny farthing', used in the 1880s, was dangerous. The arrival of a pedal driven bicycle with two equal sized wheels created new popularity for bicycles. There were several bicycle factories in Syracuse but Baldwinsville only had bicycle repair shops.

Although the bicycle seems commonplace today, it played a large role in the development of transportation.

2   Christopher, A.J. *Covered Wagon Transportation, The Baldwinsville Messenger* February 18, 1960

This is a circa 1910 image of a bicycle party at the Amos home on W. Oneida Street. The new easier to ride bicycles coupled with improved roads and streets made bicycling a popular sport before the common use of automobiles.

Its effects also extended well beyond riding down the road as shown in the following 1896 quote by Susan B. Anthony, a prominent civil rights leader and strong proponent for women's suffrage.

> *"Let me tell you what I think of bicycling. I think it has done more to emancipate women than anything else in the world. It gives women a feeling of freedom and self-reliance. I stand and rejoice every time I see a woman ride by on a wheel...the picture of free, untrammeled womanhood."*

In 1896, the Seneca Cycling Club was formed in Baldwinsville and later that year a cinder path was constructed along Cooper St. (Maple Road) toward the resorts along the west side of Onondaga Lake. In all likelihood the bicycle club was formed for the main purpose of building a more appropriate path to ride bicycles. Most roads were uneven and had ruts that made bicycle riding difficult. Bicycle riding on plank roads that were well maintained was popular because of

their relatively smooth surface. The plank road through Cicero was in good repair but not easily accessible to Baldwinsville area residents. Unquestionably the increased use of bicycles created greater demand for improved roads. Bicycle use, followed by automobiles, helped pave the way for better roads.

Bobsleds

Although bobsledding may not be appropriate for a book on transportation, since this book relates to transportation in the Baldwinsville area, it is included. During the 1880s and into the early 1900s, bobsledding down Oswego St. hill, across Genesee St. and the river bridge to as far as Downer St. was a major form of winter entertainment in Baldwinsville. The bobsleds were not anything like the bobsleds we see in the Olympics, but were large and heavy, sometimes weighing more than a ton. They often carried as many as 15, or even more, and were designed for speed.

There was friendly, and sometimes not so friendly, competition between various bobsled teams with, on at least on one occasion, a team coming from Syracuse University and another team from Utica. In addition, there was local competition. Morris Machine Works constructed a bobsled with a three inch iron pipe frame filled with moulder's sand called Ironsides. There were others, including Hercules, Vulcan, Comet and Meteor, made by other businesses or teams. Often lead was added for more weight.

On cold winter evenings a 100 gallon hogshead of water arrived on Oswego St. and young boys with sprinkler cans watered the streets, which quickly became slick with ice. Men with red lanterns manned the cross streets to stop traffic whenever a bobsled was ready to go. There was a slight curve at Elizabeth St. that tested the skills of the driver. With good conditions the sleds sometimes went as far as Grove St and on occasion reached Downer St. The lighter sleds were pulled back up Oswego St. hill by the riders but horses were used to pull the heavier sleds back up the hill. The sleds made as many as three

runs in an evening and spectators were aptly entertained as the sleds whizzed by.

There was a drum on the back of the bobsled studded with railroad spikes that the brakeman forced down against the ice and snow if an emergency occurred. It was not a sport for the weak-hearted because of the frequency of serious accidents. Some of the younger women of Baldwinsville were not deterred, however, and climbed aboard for a ride. The construction of the Barge Canal in 1908 coupled with the extension of the trolley by way of Oswego and E. Genesee Streets, ended the era of bobsledding down the Oswego St. hill.[3]

Although the immediate end of bobsledding occurred because of the trolley and Barge Canal, the arrival of motor vehicles, which is the topic of the next chapter, eliminated any future possibility of bobsledding through the four-corners of Baldwinsville.

---

3   Christopher, A.J. *Bobsled Riding, The Baldwinsville Messenger* March 29, 1962

A picture of Carl Lager's bobsled, "Meteor." Speed was important and the bobsleds often had heavy frames with extra weight added to increase the speed. Bobsledding down Oswego St. and across the river on Syracuse St. was a popular winter sport in Baldwinsville on winter weekends. Great rivalry existed as to who had the fastest bobsled. Even though brakes were applied when a dangerous situation occurred, there were often accidents due to the weight and speed of the passenger loaded sled traveling downhill.

CHAPTER 8

Motor Vehicles

Man relied on his strength, animals or the force of wind to move himself from place to place from the beginning of time until he learned that control of burning organic matter could produce power for locomotion. The first working steam engine was patented in 1698, improved by James Watt in 1769, and used successfully by Robert Fulton to power a boat in 1807. Steamboats came into general use after that date, and numerous attempts were made to power road vehicles with steam but none had major success until the late 1800s.

The development of an internal combustion engine was not possible until there was an appropriate fuel. The use of gunpowder was attempted but without success. There were a number of electric car manufacturers, and 1899 and 1900 electric automobiles outsold all other types. Steam powered cars were produced but were not generally successful. The internal combustion engine made the automobile successful. Charles and Frank Duryea produced the first gasoline powered car in the US in 1893. Many others followed in their footsteps. Henry Ford had an engine running in 1893 but it was three years before he built his first car, and he used the money from the sale of that car to build a second car. Ford built some prototypes but didn't offer another car for sale until 1903. Ransom Eli Olds had a car running in 1896 but did not sell one until 1899.

Carriage and bicycle manufacturers could see the writing on the wall, and throughout the US hundreds of these companies experimented with the production of an automobile. Beverly Rae Kimes in her book about automobiles titled, *Pioneers, Engineers and Scoundrels*, stated that 2,800 auto companies once existed. By 1930, less than 50 companies remained. James F. Bellamy in

Looking at this photograph, you might think that it is a carriage. It is a carriage that has been modified to become an automobile. Early automobile manufacturers used what was available and what they were familiar with to produce an automobile.

This is an image of a steam powered 1894 Copeland vehicle, which resembles a bicycle. Inventive minds were busy attempting to motorize familiar vehicles.

Dozens, even hundreds of kinds of bicycle style, motorized vehicles were produced around the world. The one shown here was called the Triumph Roadster.

his book, *Cars Made in Upstate New York*, names over 200 car companies in Upstate New York and notes that there were likely more than that in Metropolitan New York City. Many never produced more than a prototype and some only had an idea with drawings of a vehicle.

There were numerous automobile manufacturers in Central New York. Bellamy lists over 20 in Syracuse, and one each in Phoenix, Fulton, Manlius, Canastota, Oswego and several other area cities. Some never were able to get into production but among those that did produce automobiles were the Brennan, Century, Chase, Iroquois, Stearns, Moyer and Franklin Companies.

The Franklin was by far the most successful in the Syracuse area. The company produced 128 cars in 1903 and by 1907 it employed 1,700 men in its Syracuse factory. The financial depression of 1929 and early 1930s devastated sales, and in 1932 the Franklin Company filed for bankruptcy. It produced its last car in 1934. Harvey Moyer was a successful manufacturer of carriages who started business in the Town of Lysander. Moyer produced cars from 1911-1915 but discontinued their manufacture when he saw that he would not be able to be successful in the automotive field.[1]

As the automobile evolved from the carriage much of the nomenclature remained the same until about 1905. In fact, the common name for the first automobiles was 'horseless carriages'. The tires were reshod when the hard rubber strips on the tires needed to be replaced and new ones were glued on. The car tops were called umbrellas, and the hoods were called bonnets. Fenders were mud guards and the foot step to reach the seat was called a stirrup.[2]

The drivers of early cars needed no licenses for either the car or for driving. A few instructions were given to the buyer and away he went, scaring horses and perhaps not able to stop when necessary. There are numerous stories of the driver of a new car saying "whoa" while the car continued through the side of a building. Livery stables provided horses to bring an owner's automobile back to his barn when it broke down on the roadways.

Tony Christopher relates an early automobile story in his April 25, 1963 article, *Old-Time Automobile Experiences*, published in *The Baldwinsville Messenger*.

1 Bellamy, James F. *Cars Made in Upstate New York* p.74-107
2 Feltner, Royal *Early American Auto Industry 1869-1929* p.10

This is an image of America's first successful gasoline powered automobile made by Charles Duryea of MA in 1893. He purchased a democrat wagon, added a gasoline motor and converted it into an automobile. Two years later he won the first automobile race in the US with the car.

"Sometime around 1908, Burt Smith, local druggist, and Raymond Miller jointly purchased a used Oldsmobile from R.M. Cornwall, a Syracuse dealer. This buckboard variety two men could lift; other features corresponded. It was chain driven, steered with a tiller (lever) and rode on hard rubber tires. It was equipped with acetylene lights and a trumpet horn to clear the way. The emergency brake lever projected outside the body; had no top and sat two. On one occasion, as related by Mr. Miller, they barely reached the Phoenix Fair when the bolts came out of the springholders, separating the rear axle from the car. The chain broke and the back of the auto fell to the ground. They notified Tim Cronin at his livery stable next to the village firehouse and he came with a horse and buggy to tow them to town."

The author's father related one of his experiences in 1913 when he was walking from Plainville to school in Baldwinsville. A gentleman stopped and offered him a ride in his automobile. Every little while the car stopped and the driver had to get off, crawl underneath and put the chain that drove the wheels back on its sprocket. About the third time it happened the car's owner said to him, "Well, it's better than walking isn't it."

This is a picture of a 1902 GMC truck. The early trucks had hard rubber tires and a chain drive. Notice the horn attached to the side of the seat.

In 1901, the New York State Legislature amended the existing definition of 'carriage' to include automobiles or other motor vehicles, and all other vehicles propelled by electricity, steam, gasoline or other source of energy that operated on roads, but excluded bicycles and motorcycles. The same act required, starting April 1,1901, the owner of an automobile or motor vehicle to secure a registration certificate from the Secretary of State and pay a fee of $1. The owner's initials were required to be placed on the back of the vehicle in letters not less than three inches high. A 1903 law required the Secretary of State to assign numbers, instead of letters, to be displayed on the back of vehicles. The laws of 1910 raised fees to $5 to $25 depending upon the horsepower of the vehicle and required sets of two numbered plates be placed on cars. In 1924, New York required that the operators of all motor vehicles be licensed and began driver testing. That year there were 1,953,988 licensed drivers in New York.[3]

Arguably nothing, other than the axe, changed the landscape of the United States more than automobiles and trucks powered by internal combustion engines. The combination of roads coupled with motor vehicles has made almost any location in the country a potential site for a home, factory or business. Instead of a concentration of people, business and manufacturing in cities, and farms in rural areas, all have become mixed together. No place has this been exemplified more than in Central New York and the area around Syracuse and Baldwinsville. Houses, business, manufacturing and farms have become intermingled because of the automobile. The majority of people in Central New York leave their home, climb into their automobile, and drive five, ten or even more than twenty miles, to their work five or more times a week. There is little need for a local store or grocery because people have the means to go almost anyplace within 50 miles in less than an hour.

In 1931, in anticipation of the end of trolley service between Syracuse and Oswego, companies began to apply for approval of motor bus routes in the towns of Lysander and Van Buren. On February 21,1931, Van Buren approved the operation of Syracuse & Oswego Motor Lines, Inc. and the Ontario Omnibus Corp. to operate motor bus lines in the town.[4] The town also approved operation by the Syracuse & Rochester Bus Line and Eastern Greyhound Lines.[5] On March 9,1931, Lysander approved Syracuse & Oswego Motor Lines and Eastern Greyhound Lines to operate on selected routes in the town.[6] There were probably other bus companies

---

3   Wise, Andrew W. *The History of the Vehicle and Traffic Law* p.15-17

4   Minutes of the Van Buren Town Board, p. 152
5   Minutes of the Van Buren Town Board, p. 158
6   1931 Minute Book of the Lysander Town Board

Dr. and Mrs. Sinclair of Lysander in their Sears & Roebuck automobile of the early 1900s. The automobile has wooden wheels with hard rubber tires.

A photograph by Seth Dunbar of Carl Lager in the first automobile in the Baldwinsville area. It was a steam powered 1903 Locomobile.

that serviced the Baldwinsville area in the early years, but the author has no available information.

The Syracuse and Oswego Motor Lines was founded by W.K. Zinsmeister and operated in later years by his son Walter K. Zinsmeister who lived with his family in the Town of Lysander. In 1993, the major portion of the business was purchased by the Central New York Regional Transit Authority (CENTRO) and is still operated as part of the CENTRO system. After the sale to CENTRO, Syracuse & Oswego Motor Lines concentrated on the charter and tour business, which later became a part of Coach USA's Central New York operation.

Attempts to use a motor to power a bicycle were quite numerous in Europe during the last half of the 19th century. A Frenchman filed for the first bicycle patent in the US in 1866. Bicycles were made with motors powered by steam, alcohol and various petroleum products with limited success. In 1901, the Indian Motocycle Mfg. Co., was founded by two former bicycle racers, and in 1902 produced over 500 motorcycles. Harley-Davidson started producing motorcycles in 1903 and, out of dozens of companies producing motorcycles, by 1931 Indian and Harley were the only two remaining American manufacturers producing motorcycles commercially. Motorcycles, while far from being the major means of transportation, have increased in popularity over the years; in 2011 there were 340,000 registered in New York State.

Although many boats have motors, we seldom think of boats when discussing motor vehicles. Boats and travel on our waterways are discussed in the next several chapters.

Gertrude Kratzer, long time Town of Lysander Clerk, is seated in her father-in-law's (Rumont Kratzer) 1920s convertible. There are numerous Lysander Town Clerk's books in her handwriting stored in the Town of Lysander vault.

The Mercer family enjoying a picnic in 1928 at Mills Landing, along the Seneca River west of Baldwinsville. The automobile gave people the option of spending leisure time almost any place there were roads. Walter (Bud) Mercer, on the right, was the son of Louise McMullin Mercer for whom Mercer Park was named.

Baldwinsville Memorial Day parade in 1910. The Packard automobile belonged to Windsor Morris. In the car are the chauffer Leo Brock, Mayor George Johnson and son Alfred, Lee Failing, Marcellus Johnson, Joe Taylor, Dr. Heaton and Mr. Driscoll.

A pair of Onondaga County heavy duty snowplows circa 1930. Salt was seldom used to melt snow on the highways and these plows were needed to break through high drifts.

CHAPTER 9
Travel on the Early Waterways

Wherever possible, until roads were cut through the forests, white men traveled on New York's waterways, which were the paths of least resistance. New Amsterdam, later New York City, located at the junction of the Hudson River and the Atlantic Ocean became the 'stepping off point' to Fort Orange, later Albany, and the many lands beyond. Boats had been used as a convenient means of travel for thousands of years and were easily constructed. If water for travel was available, boats were used.

The canoes used by the Iroquois were generally either dugout or covered with elm bark and were much heavier than those covered with birch bark used by some other North American tribes. These canoes could be carried over land on portages but travel on foot over land was the generally preferred method of travel. White men often traveled on land but when large loads needed to be moved they used light vessels that could carry a good quantity of supplies and be carried or dragged between navigable bodies of water. All of their early vessels were designed to travel in shallow water to minimize travel over land.

Following are a few examples of water travel by white people in early Central New York.

- Samuel de Champlain with a company of 10 Europeans and a few hundred Native Americans, mostly Hurons who often fought with the Iroquois, traveled into central New York in 1615 attacking the Iroquois. Champlain's forces traveled by water along the eastern edge of Lake Ontario and then along its southern shore. They concealed their canoes along the shores of Lake Ontario and marched south to attack either an Onondaga or Oneida fort. (There is some difference of opinion as to the exact location of the fort.) They were unsuccessful in their attack and marched back to Lake Ontario where their canoes were still safe and traveled by water back to what is now Canada.[1]

- In 1654, Father Simon Le Moyne traveled from Montreal, up the St. Lawrence to Lake Ontario, to a fishing village of the Onondagas on the Salmon River and then through the forests to the Oneida River. From there they traveled to the Seneca River and on to Onondaga Lake where they found the salt springs, which the natives considered poisonous. Returning they traveled on the Seneca to the Oswego River, encountering the rapids at Phoenix and on to Lake Ontario to return on the St. Lawrence to Montreal.[2]

---

1   Bruce, Dwight H. *Onondaga's Centennial* p. 42-46
2   Bruce, Dwight H. *Onondaga's Centennial* p. 52-56

This is an image of a bateau, which was commonly used on New York's inland waterways into the early 1800s. (Bateau (singular) bateaux (plural)) This bateau was built in 2003 for the Schenectady County Historical Society. It is 23 feet long with a beam of five feet and is capable of carrying a ton. Normally it didn't use a sail and was powered by oars or poles (poling). This would have been the type of boat that Dr. Jonas Baldwin and his wife Betsy used in 1797 when they came through what is now Baldwinsville.

- During the Sullivan-Clinton campaign of 1779, ordered by General George Washington to destroy the Iroquois Indians who had been aiding the British during the Revolutionary War, the lakes and rivers of southern, central and western New York were used as highways to the greatest extent possible. One of the several prongs of attack used the Mohawk River, Wood Creek, Oneida Lake, Oneida River, Seneca River and Onondaga Lake. Another prong, starting with 200 flat-bottomed boats at Schenectady, used the Mohawk River, Otsego Lake and Susquehanna River to Tioga. A third prong of attack traveled up the Allegheny River to Seneca country. The main thrust started from Easton, PA over the hills to the Susquehanna River and on to Tioga. Roads had to be cut for land travel and1200 pack horses obtained to carry the supplies that were transferred from the boats at Tioga.[3]

3   New York State Division of Archives and History *The Sullivan-Clinton Campaign In 1779* p. 13-15

- Ephraim Webster, who had opened a trading post on the east side of Onondaga Creek in 1784, on a later trip to Johnstown, New York met Major Asa Danforth. They became friends and he convinced Danforth of the possibilities for business opportunities in Onondaga County. Webster requested permission from the Onondagas for Danforth to settle in their territory and permission was granted. Major Danforth set out on the Mohawk River from Johnstown to Onondaga (approximately 100 miles) in 1788 with three boatmen and two heavily loaded flat-bottomed boats. They, of course, had to portage from the Mohawk River to Wood Creek which entered into Oneida Lake. He followed the Oneida River to the Seneca River, to Onondaga Lake and to Onondaga Creek. At Onondaga Creek they partially unloaded the boats. The boats with their remaining cargo were pushed up Onondaga Creek to about one-

The Durham boat, also referred to as a Mohawk, Schenectady or other name depending upon where it was made, was larger than the bateau and was increasingly used as the inland waterways were improved. A Durham boat came to a point on each end and, although they varied in size, some were as large as 66 feet long, six feet wide, three feet deep, flat bottomed and needed but 20 inches of water when loaded. They were used to carry large loads on New York's internal waterways before the Erie Canal. They were propelled by poling and oars and could carry loads as large as 10 tons. Christmas Day, 1776, Durham boats were confiscated by General Washington to cross the Delaware River to surprise the Hessian soldiers at Trenton.

HAYING ON THE HUDSON

This is a painting of a farmer ferrying a load of hay across a river. Where bridges were not available to cross rivers, a ferry boat connected the roads on each side of the stream. Courtesy of Albany Institute of History and Art, 1968.47.98

half mile from Onondaga Valley. Meanwhile Major Danforth's son Asa and Comfort Tyler came overland driving their livestock. [4]

Rivers and lakes had long been considered public highways. In 1801, the State was divided into 20 counties and the legislature declared certain streams as public highways within some counties. In Onondaga County, portions of Nine Mile, Limestone and Butternut Creeks were declared public highways and penalties were fixed for obstructing the designated sections of these streams. [5]

When water was available for a large portion of their journey, fur traders, explorers, soldiers and settlers traveled on waterways whenever it was possible. This preference continued until paths became crude roads allowing horses and oxen to pull loads on flat-bottomed sleds or oxcarts that were more maneuverable than wagons through the forests. As roadways were further improved, a smaller portion of travel occurred on the waterways of Central New York. Short distance travel from departure to destination without portages continued but water travel with long portages was avoided. Once canals were constructed, however, water travel, especially for the transport of freight, became dominant.

4   Bruce, Dwight H. *Onondaga's Centennial* p. 184-185
5   Bruce, Dwight H. *Onondaga's Centennial* p. 217

CHAPTER 10

The Erie and Other Major Canals in Central New York

Without its natural waterways and the canals connecting them, New York would never have become the "Empire State." New York prospered like no other state during the 1800s and for over a hundred years its growth was the envy of all other states. Along the natural waterways and canals most of New York's cities and major villages developed, including New York City, Albany, Utica, Syracuse, Rochester, Buffalo, Oswego and Baldwinsville. Without question the Erie Canal was the major component in building New York into the Empire State but other smaller and lesser known canals played significant parts.

In 1702, a plea was made to New York's colonial governor Cornbury, by an Iroquois leader, requesting the removal of trees from what later became known as Wood Creek. Cornbury ordered that the creek be cleared of the trees and that use of the creek be available to everyone. In 1725, 57 canoes from Albany crossed this great carrying place at Wood Creek and returned to Albany with 738 packs of beaver and deer skins.[1] There is no record or proof but Native Americans had likely made minor improvements to canoe navigation on the New York waterways for many years.

As trade with the natives increased and white settlers moved into areas west of Rome, the first canoes were gradually replaced with bateaux, which were stronger and could carry loads up to one and one-half tons. They varied in size but were typically 18 to 24 feet long and pointed on both ends. As trade continued to increase and the waterways were improved, the bateaux were made larger.[2]

The difficulties in transversing long distances over our natural waterways before 1793 are hard to comprehend today. Traveling by water on the Mohawk River to Oneida Lake and on to Baldwinsville presented many obstacles. From Albany to Schenectady the rapids were impassable, requiring the 16 mile distance to be overland by wagon or on foot. From Albany a bateau could navigate the 58 miles to Little Falls by poling to force the boat over 57 rapids often called rifts. At Little Falls the boat had to be unloaded with both boat and cargo portaged a mile overland to the top of the falls. During the next 38 miles to Fort Stanwix at Rome the boat was forced over 22 more rapids where it again had to be unloaded and portaged two miles to Wood Creek, which was just a tiny stream, in some places narrow enough to jump over. On Wood Creek it was a 23 mile trip on log-choked shallow water, so full of turns that in one place a mile on water was traveled to advance 30 feet by land. Once a small boat reached Oneida Lake it could travel with less difficulty to the Seneca River but still had to portage at McHarrie's Rifts (Baldwinsville) and other rapids along the way. As difficult as this route was, it was the way many of our earliest settlers came to Central New York and often preferable to traveling on primitive or nonexistent roads through the wilderness.[3]

The first significant improvements to New York's natural waterways were made after the formation of the Western Inland Lock Navigation Company (WILNC) by an act of the New York State Legislature in 1792. The goal of the company was to develop an uninterrupted water transportation route from the Hudson River to Lake Ontario by way of the Mohawk River, Wood Creek, Oneida Lake and the Oneida and Oswego Rivers, and also to Seneca Lake using the Oneida and Seneca Rivers. A year after its formation the company dug 13 short canals across necks of land shortening Wood Creek by six miles. They also removed trees from the creek that continually complicated boat travel. Difficulties and cost limited WILNC's canal building success. A canal one mile long was constructed at Little Falls on the Mohawk River in 1795, but the tolls collected were barely enough to pay the canal's operating expenses. The company did make significant navigation improvements in the

---

1 Larkin, F. Daniel *New York State Canals - A Short History* p.11
2 Larkin, F. Daniel *New York State Canals - A Short History* p.12

---

3 New York State Museum *The Canal Company* p.1

Mohawk River by plowing out channels and moving rocks. In 1797, a 1.7 mile canal was constructed to bypass the portage at Fort Stanwix. A year later, near Herkimer, two troublesome rapids were removed by building a mile long canal.[4]

Improvements were sufficient to allow the firm of Eri Lasher & Co., in 1812, to run a weekly line of boats from Schenectady to Oswego, Cayuga and Seneca Falls during the open water season. The company kept wagons in readiness at Albany to transport goods and people either to Schenectady for travel by boat or alternatively by wagon to Central New York.[5]

The Erie Canal

Although the WILNC did make some improvements to the Mohawk River it ran low on money several times and even with funds from the State their attempts to

build a waterway were feeble at best. Canal proponents finally recognized that a canal of this magnitude would need to be constructed with public funds. Strong interest in a major canal from the Hudson River to the West continued and in 1808 Joshua Forman, a New York State legislator from Onondaga County, introduced a resolution to survey a canal route between the Hudson River and Lake Erie. James Geddes, also of Onondaga County, was then commissioned by the State to survey routes for a canal from Oneida Lake to Lake Ontario and from Lake Ontario to Lake Erie. Sufficient funds were not provided for a survey across land from Oneida Lake to Lake Erie but Mr. Geddes was able to include this survey in his report, and his report highly favored the latter route.[6] In 1810, a canal board of seven commissioners, appointed by the State, traveled the route recommended by Geddes' survey and agreed with his conclusion.

4   New York State Museum *The Canal Company* p.2
5   Bruce, Dwight H. *Onondaga's Centennial* p. 198

6   Clark, Joshua V.H. *Onondaga* Volume II p. 55-56

Widening and deepening the Erie Canal in the 1840s. The Erie Canal was so successful that it needed to be increased in size shortly after it was first constructed. The work being done here was similar to what occurred in widening and deepening the Baldwin Canal in Baldwinsville. Courtesy of the New York Museum of Cheese.

New York made attempts to secure financial aid from the federal government to help construct the Erie Canal but to no avail. Discussion continued regarding the feasibility of building the canal with strong views expressed both for and against.

Transportation problems during the War of 1812 provided added justification for the need to improve water transportation in Upstate New York. In 1816, a memorial (petition) was prepared by a group of distinguished citizens of Onondaga County, including Dr. Jonas Baldwin, that presented a strong case for the canal passing through Onondaga County. The memorial, which was lucid, concise and forcible was signed by over 3,000 area residents. It generously estimated the total cost of a canal at $10 million. Shortly thereafter an act was passed in the New York State Legislature authorizing a canal from the Hudson River to Lake Erie and a loan for a million dollars on the credit of the State. The middle section from Rome to the Seneca River was chosen as the first portion to be constructed. De Witt Clinton had long been a strong supporter of a canal and his advocacy for the canal won him the governorship of New York for a second term in 1817. On July 4,1817, in ceremonies at Rome, construction on the Erie Canal began.[7]

The middle section was 94 miles long and it required 3,000 men and hundreds of draft animals to toil on this Utica to Montezuma section. At Montezuma men worked in difficult conditions, often working in swampland, standing in a foot of water with many dying from malaria contracted from mosquitos. The poor working conditions slowed progress on the project. To fill the ranks, Irish immigrants were brought up from New York City. Because of the great need for men the wage rate was raised to $1.25 a day and enough workmen were obtained.[8]

In Governor Clinton's 1820 message to the state legislature, he announced that the middle section of the Erie Canal had been completed, at an average cost of $13,000 a mile. The cost of the eastern section averaged $28,000 a mile and the western section $20,000. The total cost of the original Erie Canal, including the Champlain Canal, which was built at the same time as the Erie, was over $8 million. At the same time as the middle section

was constructed, a mile and a half extension of the canal was added to reach the salt industry at Salina (near the present Carousel Mall) and to connect Onondaga Lake with the Seneca River.[9]

Sections of the Erie Canal were put into use as they were completed. When the Erie Canal was completed from Rome to Montezuma, towpaths were provided so horses and mules could furnish the power to move the boats. The first packet boat traveled on the canal on April 21, 1820, when the middle section opened. In 1823, the number of canal boats that reached Albany from the West was 1,329 and in 1827 the number had increased to approximately 7,000.[10]

One may wonder why Dr. Baldwin, who in 1808 had constructed a canal around the dam in Baldwinsville, could be a proponent of the Erie Canal since it was planned to pass a few miles south of Baldwinsville, almost certainly decreasing traffic on the Baldwin Canal. Records clearly show that when the Erie Canal opened, traffic through the Baldwin Canal became predominantly local. In addition, business growth moved away from Baldwinsville to villages along the Erie Canal leaving Baldwinsville with less opportunity for growth. Perhaps, when he supported the Erie Canal, he envisioned its path would be along the Seneca River or he may have been satisfied to have it bypass Baldwinsville with a connection through the Oswego Canal.

On October 26, 1825, a flotilla of boats entered the Erie Canal at Buffalo with Governor Clinton and numerous other dignitaries aboard, taking the inaugural 500-mile journey on the Erie Canal to New York City. They passed through Syracuse on November 1, 1825, and, upon arriving in New York City, Clinton emptied two casks of water taken from Lake Erie into the Atlantic Ocean celebrating the "Marriage of the Waters." It was the first connection of the waters from west to east. Opponents of the canal had derided it, calling it "Clinton's Ditch" and "Clinton's Folly." Governor Clinton must have received great satisfaction with the blending of those waters.

Before the Erie Canal opened, New York City's harbor had about the same tonnage as Boston and was second to Philadelphia. When the canal was completed New York's harbor soon became number one in the nation and the city blossomed from the tremendous commerce that

---

7   Clark, Joshua V.H. *Onondaga* Volume II p. 59-61
8   Larkin, F. Daniel *New York State Canals - A Short History* p.18-19

9   Clark, Joshua V.H. *Onondaga* Volume II p. 61-64
10 Bruce, Dwight H. *Onondaga's Centennial* p.222-233

Circa 1895 farmer's market along the Erie Canal in what is now Clinton Square in Syracuse. Produce came from the farms by horse and wagon and produce left the market on the wagons of peddlers and stores. Some produce also came and left by boats on the Erie Canal. Photo courtesy of OHA Museum & Research Center.

was created. Business prospered along the entire length of the canal, spread to the Midwest and provided an economic boost to the entire country. Although there were many canals constructed in the United States, the Erie Canal proved to be the greatest. It was so successful that it set off a frenzy of canal building across the United States.

In 1825, during the first year of the complete canal's operation, 185,000 tons of freight, consisting mostly of grain, flour, spirits and lumber, traveled eastward, and 32,000 tons, consisting mostly of manufactured goods, traveled to the west. The cost to transport a ton of wheat from Lake Erie gradually dropped from $100 a ton, on ox-pulled wagons, to $5 a ton on the Erie Canal.[11] By 1845, freight on the canal surpassed one million tons

and seven years later it passed two million tons. The canal freight volume peaked in 1880 when it reached over four and one-half million tons.[12]

By 1836 most of New York's productive land was settled and production in the State accounted for 70% of the major items transported on the Erie Canal. Forty years later the situation had reversed with only 30% coming from New York. Lands to the west of New York were in full production and the canal was moving their products to markets in New York City and around the world. This made the Erie Canal more vulnerable to competition from the railroads where products could be loaded on railroad cars in Chicago and other distant points and shipped without handling to New York City with its seaport. By 1880, the railroads were carrying

---

11 Larkin, F. Daniel *New York State Canals - A Short History* p.21-28

12 Larkin, F. Daniel *Essay About the Erie Canal - Erie Canal Freight* p.1

Weighlock building on the Erie Canal in Syracuse circa 1900. Line or freight boats paid for the use of the Erie Canal according to the distance they traveled and the weight of their load until the State made it a free canal in 1882 because of competition from the railroads. This building now serves as a canal museum. Photo courtesy of OHA Museum & Research Center.

Hundreds of barrels of apples at Medina, New York awaiting shipment on the Erie Canal. Canals provided the means for raw materials and manufactured goods to move to market long before the tractor trailers that we are familiar with today came into use.

more freight tonnage than New York's canals. Passenger traffic volume on the railroads had surpassed the canals many years earlier.[13]

A.J. Christopher, in an article published in the *Baldwinsville Messenger,* relates a little of a conversation with Henrietta Meloling Comerford who assisted her father on two freight boats which operated out of Baldwinsville under the name of "Edwin Meloling." He ran the boats in tandem on the Baldwin, Baldwinsville and Erie canals in the late 1800s. She stated, *"I was an all round helper to my father. When he was short handed I handled the horses and the ropes. One week I baked 22 loaves of bread, 10 tins of biscuits and two Johnny cakes. I remember one time when we went with a large*

---

13 Nostrant, Robert F. *Steam Canal Boats on the Erie Canal* p.7-10

number of other tows, down the Hudson, with a big side-wheeler moving us as a group. We drew mostly lumber and plied the full length of the Erie Canal between Albany and Buffalo." Hundreds of families like the Melolings, scattered throughout New York State, spent a large part of their lives on freight and packet boats moving goods and people from place to place around the State.

The Erie, when it opened in 1825, was only 40 feet wide at the top, 24 feet at the bottom and four feet deep but it changed New York and the entire country. Lock size and water depth limited boats to 30 tons but thousands of these boats traveling on the canal were sufficient to change the country. Almost immediately voices were calling for improvements to increase its size and permit the travel of larger boats with heavier loads. By 1862, it had been deepened to seven feet, lock size had been

A boat on the Erie Canal in Geddes being loaded with barrels of salt from one of the salt blocks (salt evaporating sheds) for transport to almost any location in the world. Photo courtesy of OHA Museum & Research Center.

Changing tow horses on a freight or line boat traveling the Erie Canal. The horses or mules that pulled the boat were housed in one end and were usually changed every six hours. Courtesy of the New York Museum of Cheese.

A major Erie Canal break occurred in Syracuse on July 30, 1907 in front of the Jacob Amos flour mill. A few years later the Erie Canal was replaced by the Barge Canal, which by-passed Syracuse. Jacob Amos also had a large flour mill in Baldwinsville. Photo courtesy of OHA Museum & Research Center.

The Erie Canal Aqueduct over the Genesee River in Rochester. Note the boats entering each end of the aqueduct, which in the photograph looks similar to a highway over a river. Aqueducts were necessary whenever the canal crossed over a river or a large stream. A smaller aqueduct was recently restored near Camillus.

increased and the canal could handle boats carrying up to 240 tons. With the abolishment of tolls in 1882, It became a free canal. Prior to that time it had earned 42 million dollars more than the total of its original cost, expense of enlargement, maintenance and operation.[14]

Competition from the railroads increased demand for the Erie Canal to be enlarged and modified to accommodate engine powered boats. It was hoped that upgrading the canal would keep it financially competitive and continue to benefit the people of New York State. Various options were explored and it was decided to enlarge it and to use natural waterways such as Oneida Lake and the Seneca River where appropriate. The result was a redesigned Erie becoming the main branch of the Barge Canal System, capable of handling large diesel powered barges. It opened in 1918 and included the Oswego, Champlain and Cayuga-Seneca Canals. Gone were the horses and mules. The original man-made canals now became a modern inland corridor featuring natural waterways linked by stretches of land cut canals. It is this Barge Canal System that continues to function today as the New York State Canal System.

The Oswego Canal

Oswego was considered for the terminus of the canal to the West from the Hudson River prior to the decision to build the Erie Canal across land to Lake Erie. England owned Canada, directly across from Oswego on Lake Ontario, and since the War of 1812 between the United States and England ended only three years before the start of the Erie Canal, there was concern about a canal seriously exposed to England's influence. Had relations with England been better or had the Americans been successful in their attacks upon Canada during the war, some speculate the canal would have ended at Oswego.

As the construction of the Erie Canal was nearing completion, a connection from it to Oswego was again considered. A connection would likely bring considerably more business to the Erie Canal by capturing the trade of residents on both sides of Lake Ontario. In addition, great quantities of salt were being produced at Syracuse and a canal to Oswego and Lake Ontario was very important for the salt industry. The State began construction of the canal from Syracuse to Oswego in 1825 and it was opened in the spring of 1829. There were 18 lift locks over the 38 miles of the canal and they were the same dimensions as those on the Erie

---

14 Finch, Roy G. *The Story of the New York State Canals* p. 4-11

Canal. About half of the distance was slack water on the Oswego River and a towpath was constructed along its side. The canal turned out to be a good investment as it was well traveled and cost less than $600,000 to build. When the Erie Canal's locks were increased in size in 1862 the Oswego Canal locks were increased to the same size.[15]

There is little question that the Oswego Canal was of significant benefit to Syracuse, Fulton and Oswego along the waterway but also to Baldwinsville and other Central New York villages and cities nearby.

The Cayuga and Seneca Canal

The Seneca River, passing through Baldwinsville originates from the northern end of Seneca Lake. Early

travelers heading west often used the Seneca River and portaged around numerous rapids along its way. The State built a canal connecting Seneca and Cayuga Lakes in 1821 while construction of the Erie Canal was in progress. The residents of the area around Geneva and Seneca Falls petitioned the State to continue the canal to connect with the Erie Canal at Montezuma in 1824. Two years later construction began and the canal was completed in 1828. There were 12 lift locks along the canal's 22 mile length and the natural course of the Seneca River was used for about half of that distance. Both Seneca and Cayuga Lakes extend over 30 miles to the South and this short canal provided access to the Erie Canal for thousands of people.[16]

Although the Seneca River wasn't improved between

15 Larkin, F. Daniel *New York State Canals - A Short History* p.49-51

16 Larkin, F. Daniel *New York State Canals - A Short History* p.51-52

A team of mules pulling a boat on the Oswego Canal approaching the Park Street Bridge in Syracuse circa 1900. Boats could travel from the Erie Canal to the Oswego Canal to the Baldwinsville Canal at Mud Lock and on to the Baldwin Canal. Photo courtesy of OHA Museum & Research Center.

Baldwinsville and Seneca Falls until the Barge Canal opened in 1918, passage on the Seneca River westward was still possible for smaller boats. A towpath along the river 10 1/2 miles from Baldwinsville to Jacks Reef had been constructed much earlier but was abandoned in 1888 because of lack of use.

Oneida Lake Canal

Oneida Lake and Wood Creek had been important parts of the waterway from Albany to the West since the time of the first Native Americans. With the opening of the Erie Canal, which did not include these waterways, they no longer were part of this important east-west water route. In 1832, area residents petitioned the State legislature for a canal from the Erie Canal to Oneida Lake. The Oneida Lake Canal Company was formed and built a four and one-half mile canal, opening in 1835, which connected the Erie with Wood Creek, two miles east of Oneida Lake. The company did not abide

by certain State requirements and was taken over by the State in 1841. With general deterioration of the canal, including its seven wooden locks, the canal was closed to traffic in 1862. A new canal was constructed from the Erie at Durhamville to Oneida Lake in 1877 but quicksand caused numerous breaks and it was closed a year later.[17]

With the construction of the Barge Canal System in 1918, and the Erie Canal now passing across the length of Oneida Lake, residents around the lake and Wood Creek again had direct access to a canal. In the next chapter the canals that had a direct effect upon Baldwinsville, including the Baldwin Canal, the Baldwinsville Canal and the rerouting of the Erie Canal through Baldwinsville will be discussed.

———————————————

17 Larkin, F. Daniel *New York State Canals - A Short History* p.57-59

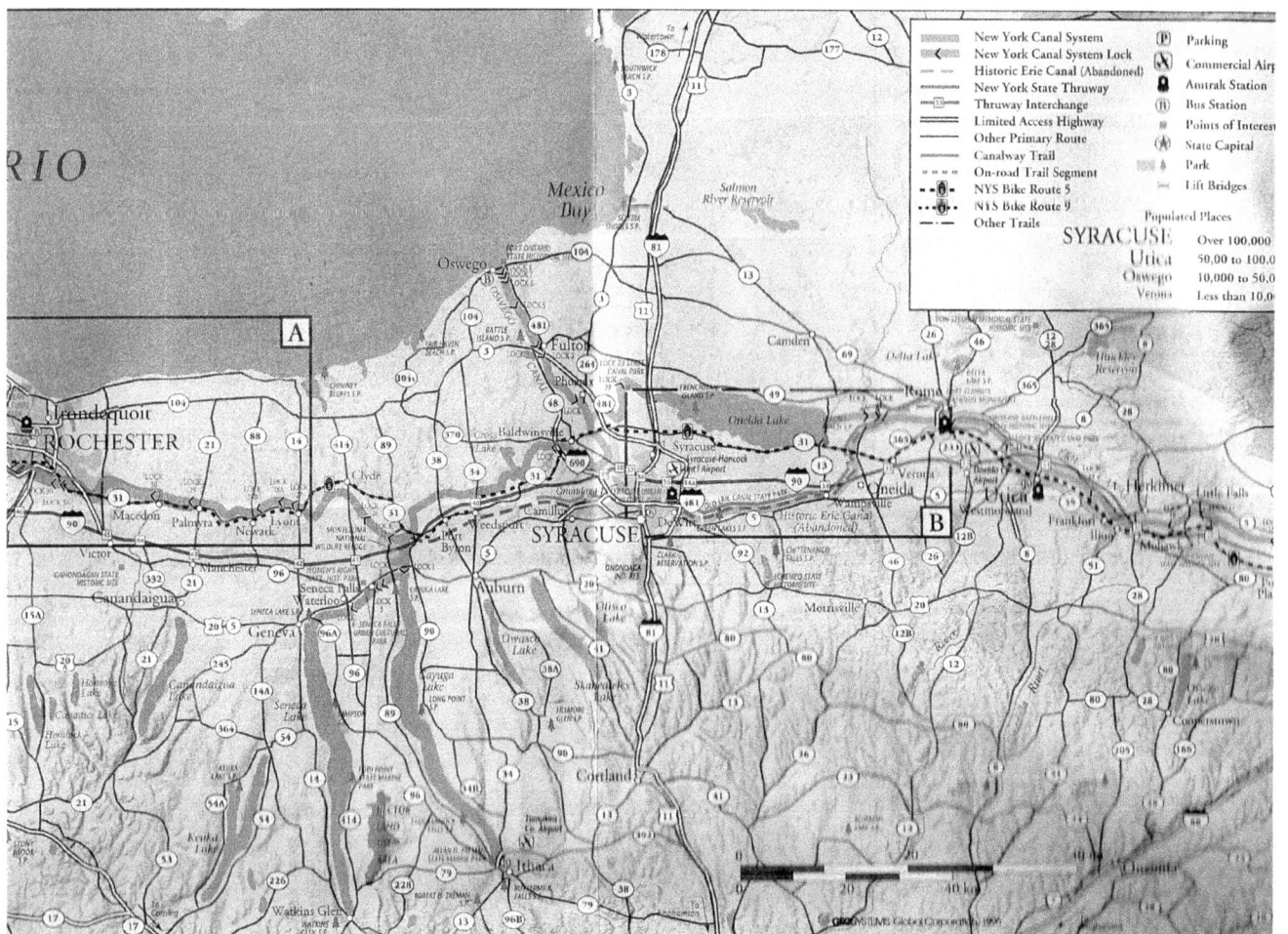

A modern map showing the paths of the Erie, Oswego, and the Cayuga-Seneca Canals making up the Central New York portion of the New York Canal System. Note how much of the natural waterways are used, including the Seneca River and Oneida Lake.

CHAPTER 11

Baldwin, Baldwinsville and Barge Canals

The Western Inland Lock Navigation Company (WILNC) indirectly had significant effects on what later became Baldwinsville. Dr. Jonas Baldwin had served as physician for workmen constructing a canal around the falls at Little Falls. With the canal completed, his services were no longer needed by the WILNC so in 1797 he set out to settle on property he owned near Ovid. Dr. Baldwin's wife was reluctant to leave the developing community at Little Falls and the doctor placated her by promising to purchase whatever property she chose along the approximately 100 mile trip to Ovid. As their boat rounded a bend in the Seneca River at McHarrie's Rifts that October morning, and they viewed for the first time the forest covered hill to the North, brilliant with fall covering, Mrs. Baldwin is said to have exclaimed, "Oh Jonas, how beautiful! If our home lay here, lonely as it is and remote from settlement, I could be happy the rest of my life."

During the several hours it took for the boatmen and John McHarrie to move their boat over the rifts, the Baldwins examined the fine wooded property north of the rifts and inquired who owned the property they wished to buy. They learned that it was owned by a man in Philadelphia and the following year Dr. Baldwin purchased the land, which is now the center of Baldwinsville.[1]

In 1807, almost ten years after Dr. Baldwin's purchase of property at McHarrie's Rifts, residents of the area submitted a petition to Dr. Baldwin outlining the waterpower possibilities at the rifts and encouraging him to build a mill. The closest mill at the time was located at Camillus requiring two days travel, which was a great inconvenience. Dr. Baldwin responded positively and soon he and Mrs. Baldwin moved to their property in Columbia, formerly called McHarrie's Rifts and later named Baldwinsville.[2]

A crew of workmen were employed by Dr. Baldwin in constructing a wing dam west of the outlet of Tannery Creek (at about what is now 34 E. Genesee St.) in preparation for the construction of a mill near Tannery Creek. The wing dam did not provide sufficient waterpower for the operation of a mill, which required a change of plans. It became necessary to place a dam across the Seneca River to obtain sufficient fall to operate waterwheels with enough power for mill operations. During construction the workmen contracted a malignant fever (malaria). Work came to a standstill until more workers could be recruited. The dam was finally completed in the fall of 1808 with the mill race and mills operating successfully.[3]

The construction of the Baldwin Dam was an amazing feat of ingenuity and cooperation. Unquestionably the time chosen to construct the dam was during a period of limited river flow during the late summer. The river's drainage basin, in 1808, was almost untouched by human development and it produced a far smaller stream than we often see today. This first dam across the river was short lived because in the following spring a large flow of water washed it away.

The unfortunate experience with the first dam required Dr. Baldwin to build a sturdier replacement dam. John McHarrie and Gabriel Tappan collaborated with him, and with the assistance of many others a new dam was put into place slightly to the west of the current dam. A large tree, five feet in diameter at its base, growing near the proposed dam, was felled. All available settlers in the area arrived with 20 teams of oxen and chains to drag the huge tree across the Seneca River to form a foundation for the new dam. Smaller logs and stones were put into place to fill any voids and raise the dam to the necessary height. The dam survived for many years but gradually became unsafe and the State started to rebuild it. In May 1894, a 60-foot section was washed away by high water,

---

1   Palmer, Miss L. Pearl *Historical Review of the Town of Lysander* Part 29
2   Palmer, Miss L. Pearl *Historical Review of the Town of Lysander* Part 29

3   Clark, Joshua V.H. *Onondaga* Volume II p. 164-165

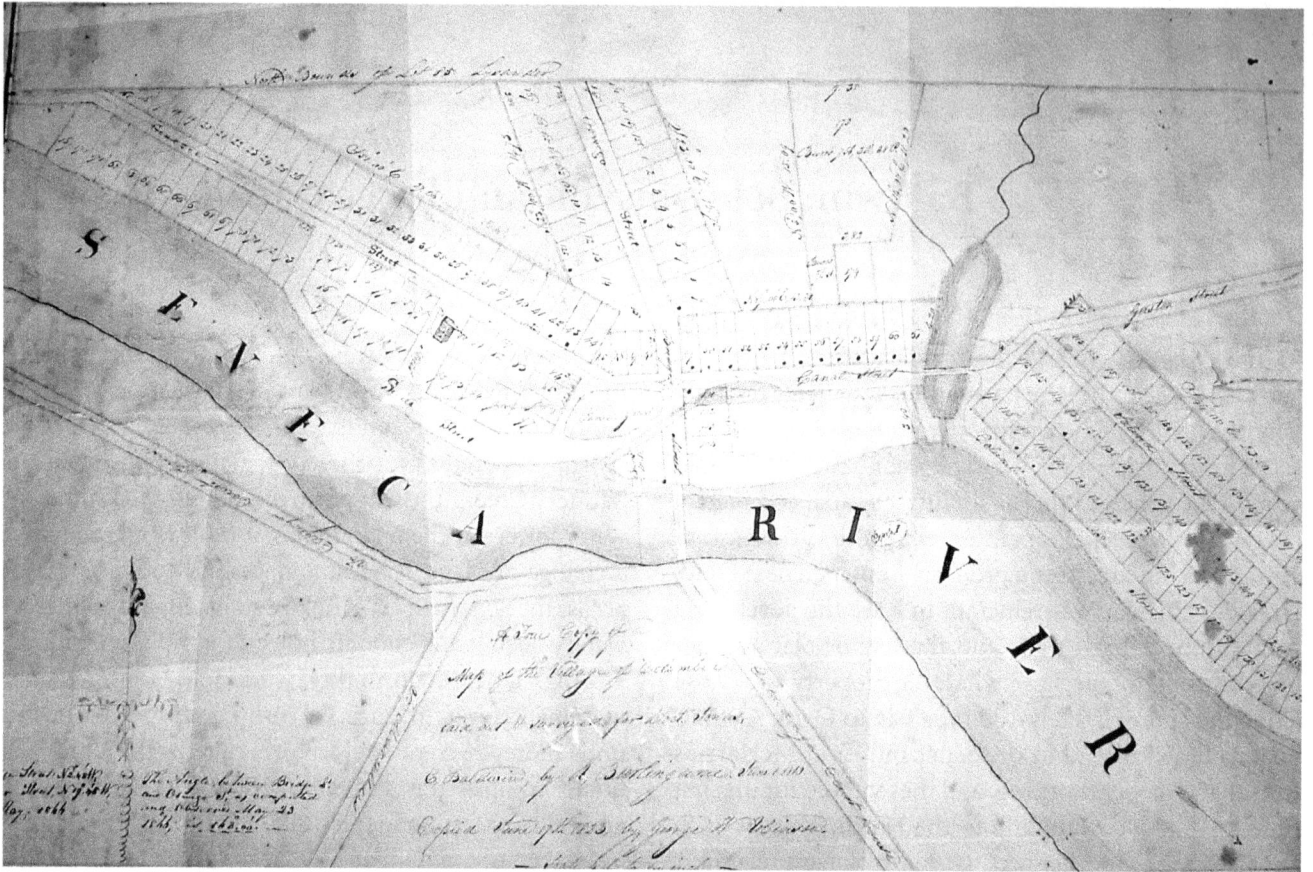

An 1810 map of the village of Columbia laid out and surveyed for Dr. Jonas Baldwin by A. Burlingame. Note the Baldwin Canal as it leaves the Seneca River to the north of the dam and re-enters the river slightly west of what we now know as Tannery Creek. The water flow from the river supplemented with water from Tannery Creek formed a millpond that furnished waterpower for Dr. Baldwin's sawmill. Some years later the Baldwin Canal was extended further east and the millpond was filled in.

reducing the river level by five feet within 24 hours. Little damage was done, however, and the State replaced the Baldwin Dam with a new stone dam slightly east of the old one.[4] Repairs have been made to the dam over the years, and a new higher cap was placed on it at the time the Barge Canal was constructed, but the old stone dam still survives, functioning well for over 100 years.

The Seneca River had been declared a public highway by the State Legislature in August 1798[5] making it necessary for Dr. Baldwin to provide for the passage of boats around his dam. In 1808, he applied to the New York State Legislature for permission to erect a dam, locks and canal. The State had previously, in 1792, granted rights to the Inland Lock Navigation Company so were unable to grant his request but Baldwin was able to purchase the water rights from Cayuga Lake to the Oneida River outlet from the company and moved ahead with the construction of the dam. Having been in their employ at Little Falls for several years, Dr. Baldwin was well known to the company. Once he had obtained the water rights, the State, in 1809, willingly granted Dr. Baldwin permission to construct the dam, locks and a canal. The State was pleased to have the rapids eliminated because it had been very difficult for boats to pass through them and it had become obvious that the WILNC had no interest in making improvements at McHarrie's Rifts. He was also given the right to collect tolls for 20 years on all boats passing through the canal and locks.

In Chapter 54 of the Laws of 1809, the State made some specific requirements of Dr. Baldwin. He was permitted to raise the water level with his dam at the rifts a maximum of seven and one-half feet. It also specified that at least 30 feet of the dam should be constructed to admit the passage of rafts and boats down the river. To allow this passage of rafts and boats downstream, the dam was constructed with an apron of a slight pitch

---

4   Hall, Edith *History of Baldwinsville* p. 65
5   Scisco, Louis Dow *Early History of the Town of Van Buren* p. 12

leading from its crest to the lower water level allowing boats without loads to travel downstream without passing through the canal. Baldwin was also required to provide sufficient canal depth for loaded boats drawing two feet of water. The State required that the lock be at least 12 feet wide and a minimum of 77 1/2 feet between gates. It also permitted Baldwin the right of eminent domain. In addition, it granted the right to take and make use of the water retained by the dam for the use of mills and hydraulic works or any other use which the same capable of being applied, upon land owned by Baldwin, his heirs and assigns, and that these privileges and advantages should continue for 20 years. By later statutes, these privileges and advantages were continued until 1850. The State, using Chapter 153 of the Laws of 1850, took over the Baldwin Canal [6] in response to a petition of some 400 residents.[7]

6   Hall, Edith *History of Baldwinsville* p. 26
7   Palmer, Miss L. Pearl *Historical Review of the Town of Lysander* Part 99

Building the Baldwin Canal was not a simple task. It was first laid out from near the east end of River St. and headed east along the south side of what is now E. Genesee St., reentering the Seneca River near the west end of Lock St. There was little in its path other than trees and stumps from trees previously cut. Digging the canal was almost entirely with pick, shovel and wheelbarrow. Oxen and chains helped remove stumps, and oxen would likely have been used to pull a plow to move dirt from the center toward the sides of the canal. Oxen also may have been used to pull dirt, with a scraper fashioned from a split log, from the center of the canal to the sides. The canal was designed for boats with a two-foot draught and was dug to a depth of four or five feet to allow clearance and space for silt deposit. The canal was 12 feet wide at its bottom and a barrier of logs and stones lined both sides of the canal. The bank on the north side was leveled for use as a towpath. The single lock was constructed of wood.[8]

8   Christopher, A.J. *The Baldwinsville Messenger* Anecdotes From Baldwin Canal, June 10, 1965

The Baldwin Canal wooden lock at the canal's east end by Lock St. The Baldwin Canal was constructed in 1808 and was in active use for more than a century. It was used for the shipment of commercial goods, to and from Baldwinsville's numerous industries, as well as passengers.

The Wilkins or Seneca Mill was erected in 1854. The building stood between the river and the Baldwin Canal at 34 East Genesee Street. Water from the Baldwin Canal turned the waterwheels that powered the mill. Notice the canoe in the canal and the wagon on the bridge. The bridge is elevated to permit boats to pass underneath.

When the canal was first constructed a large mill pond was excavated east of Tannery Creek (43 E. Genesee St.) to provide water for Baldwin's mills. In later years the canal was extended along the south side of Lock St. increasing its length to a total of about three-quarters of a mile. Other changes were made to the canal over the years including new locks, widening, deepening and moving it slightly further south but still parallel to E. Genesee St.

In 1819-20 Dr. Baldwin turned over his remaining interests in Baldwinsville to his sons Stephen W. and Harvey Baldwin. They made additional improvements to the canal, bridge and dam.[9]

In 1824, Stephen Baldwin purchased 13 acres including the land on the south side of the river north of Water St. extending to the river. He planned to build a canal similar to the one on the north side, extending from above the dam to some point below it. In 1825, part of the canal was constructed but it did not extend across Syracuse St. to the river even though permission had been granted by the State. The portion constructed did provide access to the Seneca River and to the existing Baldwin Canal north of the river for businesses located along its sides.[10]

Railroads took much of the freight and passenger business from the canals after the middle 1800s but both the Baldwin Canal and the Baldwinsville Canal, described below, continued to have considerable traffic into the early 1900s. Usage of the Baldwin Canal gradually

9 Bruce, Dwight H. *Onondaga's Centennial* p.744

10 Scisco, Louis Dow *Early History of the Town of Van Buren* p. 26

decreased and came to a standstill a few years after the Barge Canal came through Baldwinsville. The old swing bridges were replaced with permanent flat bridges to reach the businesses on the island created by the Baldwin Canal. Water in the old canal became stagnant and sometimes smelly, and debris began to accumulate in it. Some manufacturers had continued to draw water from the canal for power and their ownership of water rights had to be negotiated. After a long process the State relinquished rights of the canal to the village, and 1965 brought an end to the Baldwin Canal which had served the community well but had become an eyesore in its last years. The old Baldwin Canal, now filled with dirt and resting peacefully under a busy village, offers only an occasional clue to its former existence. The most notable clue is the bridge on Oswego St., barely noticeable, and the walkway underneath connecting parking lots on each side of the street.

Baldwinsville Canal

In 1831, the connection to the Seneca River to Baldwinsville (Baldwinsville Canal) was improved to accommodate boats of the Erie and Oswego Canals and in 1836 steps were taken to join the canal with the main system. $4,000 was appropriated to construct a tow path from Mud Lock, at the junction of the Oswego Canal and the Seneca River, to Baldwinsville. Two years later the appropriation was raised to $15,000 and the towpath was completed in 1839.[11] Most of the appropriation was used in constructing the 5.36 mile towpath along the north side of the river. A large portion of the cost was a float bridge 367 feet long by 19 feet wide, used as part of the towpath east of Baldwinsville and crossing the end of a pond near where the railroad crosses the river today. The float bridge was treacherous for the horses whenever it was wet, and occasionally a horse fell into the river or received injuries.[12]

---

11 Palmer, Miss L. Pearl *Historical Review of the Town of Lysander* Part 99

12 Christopher, A.J. *The Baldwinsville Messenger* Old Float Bridge at Frawley's Pond, July 6, 1967

This pleasure boat rests peacefully on the Baldwin Canal slightly to the rear of the current Key Bank at 10 E. Genesee St. This image provides a good perspective of the prominence of the Canal as it passed through the center of Baldwinsville.

There was also a towpath along the Seneca River to the West, ten and one-half miles to Jack's Reef, which was abandoned in 1888 because of disuse.[13] This section of the Seneca River had been used to float logs, firewood and lumber down it, but once the majority of trees had been harvested the activity ceased. In addition, until the Barge Canal was opened in 1918, the river had numerous sandbars and shallow areas over bed rock that made it dangerous for larger boats.

In the early 1840s the Orion, a packet boat drawn by a team of horses, traveled the 13 mile route from Baldwinsville to Syracuse daily except for Sunday. Horse drawn boats continued to be used on the Baldwinsville Canal into the early 1900s but were gradually replaced by steam packets in the 1880s. Walter D. Herrick, a local innkeeper, ran one of the first steam-powered freight boats between Baldwinsville and Syracuse but discontinued it for lack of profit. This boat carried passengers, charging thirty-seven and one-half cents each way, and five cents per hundred weight for freight. The approximately 13 mile trip to Syracuse took three hours. When the canal closed each November because of freezing, two men, Hall & Lusk, started running a stage on Van Buren Road to Syracuse on a daily basis. The stage left Baldwinsville at nine in the morning and returned by nightfall.[14]

---

13 Christopher, A.J. *The Baldwinsville Messenger* Exit - The Baldwin Canal, June 3, 1965

14 Christopher, A.J. *The Baldwinsville Messenger* Seneca Early Navigation Way, March 5, 1970

An 1860 map of Baldwinsville by Homer D.L. Sweet. It provides an excellent perspective of the village and clearly shows the location of the dam, bridge and Baldwin Canal in relation to the Seneca River.

With the Erie and Oswego Canals connecting with the Baldwinsville Canal, which connected to the Baldwin Canal, Baldwinsville was a busy port. The arrival and departure of various boats, some horse-drawn, others steam-driven, and the cargos they carried were listed each week under the 'Port of Baldwinsville' column on the front page of the *Gazette* newspaper. The shipping news for the first week of May 1880 listed the following arrivals: *E.E. Frost*, 4,500 bushels of wheat for Hotaling and Frazee Mills; *Stella*, 114 tons of plaster stone for Frazee Plaster Mill; *Joe Hooker* of Elmira, 128 tons of coal for J.C. Miller Co. Departures were: *Jacob Amos, Jr.* 12,000 feet of lumber from the Taggart sawmill. The *Jacob Amos, Jr.* made several trips that week carrying 114 tons of flour and feed from the Hotaling, Mercer and Frazee mills. During the same week there were other vessels carrying passengers and a variety of merchandise.[15] Records by Charles Brannock, lock tender on the Baldwin Canal in 1895, showed that 744 lockages were recorded that year.[16]

With a number of village businesses, unloading a small boat was simply extending a couple of planks from the canal boat to the shore and unloading or loading freight. Other businesses that were dealing with large shipments, including the mills, needed special freight docks for loading and unloading. Bridges over the canal were often required for employee access and for freight shipments by land. The most obvious bridge was the one carrying traffic on Syracuse and Oswego Streets on the main north-south highway, which was replaced several times over the life of the canal.

A float bridge west of the current railroad bridge. It was constructed in approximately 1845 on the north side of the Seneca River to serve as part of the towpath for the Baldwinsville Canal extending from Mud Lock, at the Oswego Canal, to the Baldwin Canal. Originally there was no rail on the side toward the Seneca River. When the bridge was wet it was dangerous for both the tow horses and drivers because it was slippery. The float bridge was 19 feet wide and 367 feet long, and cut across what was known as Frawley's Pond. At one time there was also a towpath extending along the Seneca River to Jack's Reef. Photo courtesy of OHA Museum & Research Center

The author remembers several others, one passing over the canal to the old Frazee Mill at the foot of Virginia St., another crossing the canal a little further west to Tappan Lumber Company, formerly the site of the Syracuse and Oswego Railroad yards and a third crossing the canal to reach the American Knife Company near the west end of Lock St.

Old pictures of Baldwinsville show a permanent wooden bridge over the canal to the Wilkins Mill, which was constructed at an earlier date and located near the

15 Christopher, A.J. *The Baldwinsville Messenger* 'Port of Baldwinsville' Once Figured in Canal Commerce, January 27, 1966
16 Christopher, A.J. *The Baldwinsville Messenger* Unique Bridges Once Spanned Baldwin Canal, January 19, 1967

west end of Lock Street. This high bridge provided an advantage as boats could pass under it day or night. Several bridges were swing bridges that had to be opened during the day when a large boat passed through the canal. Normally these bridges were left open at night when the business was not in operation.

The path of the 1918 Barge Canal, when it was completed through Baldwinsville, followed the Seneca River and completely replaced the Baldwinsville Canal. The Baldwinsville Canal had been a real asset to Baldwinsville making it possible for boats plying the Erie and Oswego Canals to have direct access to the Baldwin Canal and the businesses in Baldwinsville.

Barge Canal

The year 1907 brought the massive Barge Canal construction project to Baldwinsville with its relatively peaceful Seneca River and little Baldwin Canal. With the decision made to use natural waterways where possible, the dam at Baldwinsville made the construction of Lock 24 necessary, causing the loss of many businesses on the south side of the river and several years of disruption while the canal and lock were constructed. After a decade of construction, the Barge Canal officially opened to traffic on May 15, 1918. No one is living today that witnessed the announcement of the canal coming to Baldwinsville and its construction but it must have been the biggest piece of news to hit the community to date. Imagine the optimism of some people contemplating the massive canal with its opportunities for manufacturing, business and jobs coming to their community, in contrast to the disappointment of others facing loss of their businesses or homes and disrupted lives.

Because of the significant impact of the Erie Canal portion of the Barge Canal System passing through Baldwinsville, it is important to review the causes for the relocation and some of the changes that took place. The Barge Canal System was a huge undertaking for the State. It consisted of major upgrades to the Erie Canal, which was about 340 miles in length; the Champlain 63 miles; the Oswego 24 miles, and the Cayuga and Seneca 27 miles. These canals, along with the Hudson River and lakes forming part of the system, totaled more than 800 miles. The total cost, for expenses through 1924, was a little over $170 million. There were 57 locks with a usable space of 300 by 44 and 1/2 feet that provided capacity for boats carrying as much as 2,000 tons. The canal rose from sea-level at Troy to 420 feet at Rome, dropping to

363 feet at the Oswego River (the level below the dam at Baldwinsville) and back up to 565 feet elevation at the Niagara River. There were 306 highway and railroad bridges passing over the Barge Canal.[17]

Even before the 1870s, New York State recognized the Erie Canal had serious competition from the railroads. By 1862 the canal had been deepened and larger locks constructed permitting boats to carry up to 240 tons compared to the maximum of 30 tons on the original Erie Canal. In 1869, the New York Central and the Pennsylvania railroads were completed to Chicago. Competition between the railroads decreased freight rates to the point that the railroads almost went bankrupt and reduced Erie Canal traffic substantially. In 1882, by a state-wide vote for a constitutional amendment, the Erie Canal was made a free canal in an attempt to increase its freight traffic. Improvements continued to be made to the Erie Canal by increasing its capacity to carry boats with larger loads. But freight traffic on the Erie continued to decrease and there was serious concern that the New York City harbor might lose the export grain trade coming from the Midwest as well as its business derived from production and supplies produced and needed by industries in cities along the Erie Canal corridor.[18]

Later a thorough study determined that a canal following the general path of the Erie Canal and designed for large barges was a better choice than a canal through the St. Lawrence River to the Great Lakes capable of carrying ocean going ships. The study found that ships constructed for ocean service could not be operated at an advantage and it would be cheaper to transfer cargos from barges at ports on the ends of the canal.[19] There is no question that the importance of an interior State canal to New York City and to the multitude of other cities and villages along its route played a critical part in making the decision.

About a half century later, in 1959, five years after it was authorized by Congress, the St. Lawrence Seaway, which could accommodate oceangoing vessels, was opened. Canada had been a proponent of the project for many years because of its need for hydroelectric power as

17 Finch, Roy G. *The Story of the New York State Canals* p. 15-26
18 Whitford, Noble E. *History of the Barge Canal of New York State* p. 537-538
19 Finch, Roy G. *The Story of the New York State Canals* p. 9-11

A small steam engine with dump cars hauling excavation material from the digging of the Barge Canal in Baldwinsville, circa 1908. The material is being loaded on a dump scow for moving and filling marsh areas along the Seneca River.

well as its use as a canal. Once the Seaway was opened, commercial traffic on the Barge Canal rapidly declined. Worldwide commerce would have prospered more if instead of the Barge Canal, a canal had been constructed in the St. Lawrence at the turn of the century. In the shorter view of time, unquestionably the Barge Canal did provide greater benefits to New York than a canal through the St. Lawrence.

An editorial in the August 24,1899 *Gazette & Farmers' Journal* stated *"a new canal, which would benefit Baldwinsville is seriously being considered. A change in the route of the Erie Canal from Newark to Syracuse, passing through Baldwinsville on the Seneca River, would increase the water flow and the available horsepower."* (Using water from Lake Erie to feed water to the canal was under consideration then.) It went on to say, *"the removal of rocks, logs and grass in dredging the canal would make the river more desirable for pleasure boats."* Little did that writer anticipate the total change in the canal's use that would occur a hundred years later with the canal becoming essentially a recreational waterway.

By a statewide vote in 1903, the people of New York

decided to enlarge the Erie Canal with the construction of what became known as the Barge Canal. The fact that the canal was designed for large freight carrying barges was the reason for its name. Studies determined it would be better to use the lower natural water courses available rather than an artificial channel along higher ground similar to the Erie Canal's path from Syracuse to Buffalo. This decision moved the path of the Barge Canal to Baldwinsville on the Seneca River, a few miles north of the old Erie Canal.

Discussion concerning whether an improved Erie Canal with barges, a canal to accommodate ocean ships or the use of railroads was the most desirable method of moving freight from the ocean to the Midwest continued. The January 19,1905 *Gazette and Farmers' Journal* told of legal action, testing the constitutionality of the Act authorizing the canal by various parties with railroad support holding up actual construction. The estimated cost of connecting Oneida Lake and the Seneca River was over $5 million and the October 4,1907 *Syracuse Journal* reported that Stewart, Kerbaugh & Shanley received a contract for the 43 miles of construction between Mosquito Point (near Weedsport) and Brewerton for $5

A 1920 photograph of barges passing through Lock 24 of the Barge Canal, at the water level below the dam, in Baldwinsville. Mercer Milling Co. is in the upper right and the paper company smokestack and buildings are in the upper center.

million. It required moving seven million yards of dirt.

In Baldwinsville the first dirt to construct the Barge Canal was moved on June 8, 1908. The State made contracts with large construction companies who sub contracted portions with smaller contractors. Stewart Brothers, later referred to as James Stewart & Co., was the contractor for the lock and excavation extending from the west end of paper mill point to what is referred to as John Hirzel's camp at the foot of Downer St.

Today, none of us can fully comprehend the magnitude of the effort involved in moving buildings and constructing the Barge Canal through Baldwinsville. All of the buildings on the south side of Marble St, the north side of Water St. and several other buildings along Syracuse St. were moved or torn down. An article in the June 25,1908 *Gazette & Farmers' Journal* helps paint a clearer picture of the disruptions many people experienced.

"The work on the Barge Canal contract here in the village is now well started. The steam shovel, which was put into operation last Wednesday just east of the D.L. & W. R. R. freight tracks, has continued work up through to within 150 feet of Syracuse St. and has excavated a big ditch about 40 feet wide. The shovel has been taken back to the starting point and has begun a fresh cut, alongside and to the south of the first one. The buildings which have been taken by the State are now nearly all out of the pathway of the canal up to within 100 feet of Syracuse St.

Scott Brothers, the contractors of the barge canal work, have purchased from Aaron P. Clark the building on the north side of Marble St. known as the "cheese factory," which is to be moved off or torn down to make room for the Hotel Van Buren, which they will move at once onto the site now occupied by the Clark building. Charles Hoffman of Syracuse has been given the contract for moving the hotel, which will be done as soon as possible."

Contractor J.P. McCarthy has started the work of preparing a foundation for the Baker & Tappan store building, which has been purchased by George Donovan and which is to be moved across the street to the new foundation just north of Mr. Donovan's dwelling in Syracuse St. (23 Syracuse St.)

The village water commissioners, the board of trustees and Scott Brothers held an informal meeting Tuesday night to form plans for taking care of the large water main in Syracuse St. which will have to be moved. The water pipe in question is one of the principle mains in the village, being the one connected to the pipe which crosses the river just above the railroad bridge. The work will have to be done so that there will be no interruption of supplying the water throughout the system and plans are being made with this in view. As at present planned, a new line is to be laid from Water St., near the Clark & Mercer roadway, through the site of the livery stable, which is now being torn down, and connected to the main running down Marble St. This will take care of the water supply until the new barge canal bridge is built, when the pipes will be placed on top of the new structure.

Among the many pieces of property condemned for barge purposes is the transformer station of the Niagara Mohawk Power Company, located on the foot of Downer St. The land on which the station is located is required for dumping the earth excavated by the steam shovel. The station will eventually probably have to be moved but not immediately."

The *Gazette & Farmers' Journal* provided regular updates regarding Barge Canal operations over the next several years. A quote from their July 23, 1908 paper states, "*The lock will accommodate two canal boats or barges each 150 feet long, at one time. The lock will have an 11 foot lift when the work is completed.*" (Fifteen inches was added to the height of the dam.) "*The space between the present power canal and the lock will be used for a roadway landing to the paper mill.*" (The power canal was a dead end canal extending from the river on the west and ending before it reached Syracuse St.) "*The old cellars of the Baker & Tappan grocery store and of the Behling building area are to be filled in at once, to permit the laying thereon of the Lake Shore Trolley tracks, so that trolley cars can pass around the construction work of the new bridge to be built.*"

From the *Gazette & Farmers' Journal* of August 6, 1908:

"*An immense big ditch nearly 200 feet wide has been dug out and two cuts have now been made through Syracuse St. The trolley tracks have been thrown over to the west of Syracuse St. and a road has been built along side for wagons and teams, and a sidewalk for pedestrians.*

An impressive idea of the amount of earth that has been excavated for the canal can be gained by a visit to the dumping places where the dirt is unloaded from the dumping trains. Thousands of cubic yards of earth have already been placed on the two dumping sites so far used. One of the dumps is located on the river bank in the rear of E.E. Wells property and the other is further south at the foot of Downer St."

The dirt excavated for the Barge Canal and Lock 24 in Baldwinsville improved Baldwinsville by filling in a large area of swamp land between Meadow St. and the river. From its very beginnings, Baldwinsville had disease-bearing mosquitos breeding in the swamp lands that had made the construction of the Baldwin Canal a formidable task.

The construction of Lock 24 disrupted the lives of many Baldwinsville residents as well as its business community. An article in the June 27, 1909 *New York New York Sun* told of claims against the State totaling $250,000 by Morris Machine Works, Frazee Milling Co. and Penn Spring Works because the appropriation by the State of lands carrying the rails and the road bed of the D.L. & W. deprived them of freight facilities.

A mile west of Baldwinsville, at a location on the river called High Banks, it was necessary for James Stewart & Co. to use a drill boat to blast the rock at the bottom with dynamite to obtain the necessary depth of 14 feet. A large dipper dredge was used near the Mills cottage (Mills Landing, four miles west of Baldwinsville) where the excavated material was loaded on large scows that were pulled up the river with a tug boat and dumped in deep water. Both scows of a capacity of 500 yards and dipper dredges were made by the Stewart Company on the flats near Hirzel's camp that had been filled in by Scott Bros. canal work. A sawmill was also constructed on the same site to saw the lumber needed to construct these vessels.[20] James Stewart & Co. believed that they had completed their portion of the canal contract in the Baldwinsville area three years earlier in July of 1915 but was advised by the State that dirt had been

---

20 *Gazette & Farmers' Journal* October 20, 1910

A circa 1920 photograph of barges, at the water level above the dam, going through Lock 24. Mercer Milling Co. is on the left and the canal bridge on Syracuse St. is in the background.

inappropriately deposited along the river bank two miles west of Baldwinsville and that it must be removed.

With their work on the canal completed, James Stewart & Co. saw the opportunity to build barges for the US government on its yards at the foot of Water St. where it had just finished building dredges and scows for its canal contract. It was early in 1918, with World War I in progress, and the company obtained a contract from the government to build 30 lighterage barges each 100 feet long by 37 feet wide. (These boats were similar to barges and were used to off-load larger boats anchored away from a dock.) The company advertised for 400 men to help build the barges and offered unusually high wages to secure the needed help. The contract only lasted a few months because the War ended. During the period of construction every hotel and boarding house

in Baldwinsville was filled with workmen and some private homeowners took boarders.[21]

About eight miles west of Baldwinsville there was major construction at a location known as the "State Ditch." In 1854, an excavation had been made between Cross Lake and the Seneca River bypassing Jacks Reef and shortening the Seneca River by several miles. Its purpose was to help drain the lands to the West including the Montezuma marshes and Cross Lake. It was a relatively shallow trench and would have been navigable only during high water levels and by smaller boats. An advertisement in the *Syracuse Standard* of November 22, 1854 stated, *"Wanted 500 laborers at Jack's Reef on Seneca River in Onondaga County, immediately. Liberal*

---

21 Christopher, A.J. *The Baldwinsville Messenger* Barges Built in Baldwinsville, January 16, 1969

wages will be paid and constant employment given for at least two years by Wm. Baldwin & Co. contractors." This excavation was before mechanization and the effort was accomplished by men and oxen.

This ditch was substantially widened and deepened to provide a channel for large boats when the Barge Canal was constructed. The cut was through rock, and large quantities of dynamite, transported by horse and wagon from the railroad at Memphis a few miles away, were used to blast the rock. Soft coal, to fuel the steam shovel and a stationary boiler, which powered steam drills for drilling holes in the shale for the dynamite, was also transported from the railroad with horse and wagon. About 10 acres of woodland was cut to make a place for the spoil from the excavation.

The author had the opportunity to know Glen Bratt, who lived with his parents next to the Canal, and also to read the project superintendent's daily log of the work on the excavation. A narrow gauge railroad transported the excavated dirt and dumped it on land south of the ditch. The railroad cars were side-dumping and were pushed up a trestle by a small steam locomotive. A village cookhouse was constructed for cooking and serving the workers' meals, and straw was purchased from Mr. Bratt to fill their ticks (large bags which served as mattresses). The steam shovel excavated the canal by making several passes, a few feet deep each time, over its approximately one mile length. It took several years of six days a week, ten hours a day work to dig the canal. When the steam shovel operated near the Bratt Farm's barn, a large pump was hooked to a pipe from the river to keep the barn's shingles wet, and prevent sparks from the soft coal setting the barn on fire.

After the canal was dug, a ferry was used to cross the canal until a bridge was constructed. Glen Bratt related a story of an incident occurring in about 1910, probably not uncommon at ferry crossings. Fred Meaker, a neighbor of the author, had a load of potatoes he was hauling to Syracuse on a set of bobs pulled by horses. There was a steep slope down to the ferry. The horses went directly down onto the ferry and, once on, braced themselves stopping quickly to not go over the front of the ferry into the water. Unfortunately the ferry was not tied securely and the force of the horses, stopping quickly, pushed the ferry out into the canal allowing the back end of the bobs to go into the water and dumping the potatoes into the channel. Another fact of interest,

only slightly related to transportation, is that before the Barge Canal was dug, fishermen used to set traps for eels at the end of the 'State Ditch'. The eels were large and were shipped in barrels to New York City where they were considered a delicacy.

In the fall of 1915 there was a statewide referendum to increase the amount of money for the canal construction because costs had exceeded the original estimates. An editorial in the October 28,1815 *Gazette & Farmers' Journal* urged the voters to approve the increase. It stated that the canal would save millions of dollars in freight costs and that it should be completed.

There was a great deal of concern by many people regarding the potential success of the rerouted Barge Canal. An article in the February 29,1916 *Syracuse Post Standard* stated that the canal could not be successfully operated and the river still be able to furnish sufficient waterpower for Penn Spring Works, American Knife Works, Frazee Milling Co., Mercer Paper Co. (likely a misprint and was referring to Mercer Milling Co.),and Hoffman Paper Mills to operate.

The Barge Canal was completed and officially opened in 1918. Construction continued at various points along the canal including grain elevators at Buffalo and Oswego. On March 30, 1922, an article in the *Gazette & Farmers' Journal* stated that canal repair shops were going to be located in Baldwinsville on land owned by the State. A large brick building was constructed and some repair work was done at this site but over time the work dwindled and was moved to canal shops in Syracuse. Also in 1922, a Taintor gate was constructed across the fore-bay of the Seneca River Power Company to give the State control of the water level on the river. This Taintor gate is still in use today helping control the river's water level.

In a conversation with lock master Andrew Derby of Baldwinsville in the fall of 2011, he stated, *"Lock 24 is the second busiest lock on the Barge Canal with approximately 2,500 pleasure craft passing through the lock annually. When the Barge Canal was originally constructed between 1903 and 1918, it was the largest public works project in New York State up to that time. Its original use was designed for freight and to replace the Erie Canal, which was unable to handle the larger boats that were being constructed then. The number of boats carrying freight on the Canal decreased over time and there haven't been any boats carrying freight passing* through Baldwinsville in several years." Lockmaster Derby stated that some boats still carry freight through the Oswego portion of the Canal, to and from Lake Ontario, but originate east of Baldwinsville.

Derby also stated, *"The canal system not only is for boats but is critical in controlling the water level of the Seneca River and nearby lakes. The Baldwinsville area rests in what is called the Oswego Basin encompassing a drainage area over 5,000 square miles extending as far west as Canandaigua. Normal water levels at Baldwinsville are 374 feet above sea level above the dam and 364 feet below the dam, which are the normal navigational levels. At Baldwinsville, north of the dam and next to Brookfield Power, the Taintor water control gate, installed in 1922, still is opened and closed to help maintain the water above the dam near the desired 374 foot level. There is usually a water control structure at each dam along the Canal."*

During the canal's initial years, substantial freight traffic, including fuel, grain, manufactured goods and a multitude of other items, traveled on its waters. With the passage of time, greatly improved roads and the increased use of tractor trailers to haul goods directly from the door of the producer to the door of the user, traffic on the canal gradually decreased. Pipelines for the transport of oil all but eliminated the need for barges to carry fuel on the canal.

In 1992, the Barge Canal's operation was transferred from the auspices of the New York State Department of Transportation to a division of the New York State Thruway Authority. Today, what was called the Barge Canal, is known as the New York State Canal System consisting of the Erie, Oswego, Champlain and Cayuga-Seneca Canals. Although the section passing through Baldwinsville was never part of the original Erie Canal, there was access from it to Baldwinsville's Baldwin Canal, which was opened more than a decade earlier. With this in mind, it is appropriate that Baldwinsville is now on the Erie Canal.

A great variety of boats traveled New York State's natural waterways and canals. The next chapter describes a few of these boats.

Circa 1970 photograph taken during the "Blessing of the Fleet." There are probably 50 or more motor powered pleasure craft taking part in the ceremony. The picture portrays the main use of the Barge Canal since the mid 1950s.

CHAPTER 12

Boats on the Waterways

The first boats on our waterways were the canoes of the Native Americans. The canoes were either dugout from a log or elm bark fastened to a frame. Birch bark was not generally available in Central New York so elm was the favored cover for the canoe. The dugout canoes were durable but heavier and time consuming to make. Prior to the arrival of the white man, the Native Americans had only stone tools so much of the hollowing of the log was with fire and scraping the charred wood away. It took many firings to form the canoe. The white man could make a dugout canoe much easier and quicker using his steel tools. Explorers, traders and settlers from Europe were familiar with boat building and seldom made dugouts once appropriate tools were available.

The boat used on our inland waterways after the canoe, and almost certainly the kind used by Dr. Jonas

Baldwin when he came through McHarrie's Rifts (later Baldwinsville) in 1797, was a bateau. The bateau was a flat-bottomed boat with a raked bow and stern and flaring sides. This style of boat had been commonly used by the French explorers. The size varied but a typical bateau was twenty-three feet long by five feet wide and had capacity of about a ton. Two or three people could operate it and it was powered by poling or oars. It needed to be light enough to be carried around falls and rapids at portages. At each portage the bateau had to be unloaded and then both boat and goods carried past the obstacles to be reloaded before continuing travel.

As the waterways were improved to permit larger boats that could carry larger loads, the Durham came into use. It was a long, flat-bottomed boat pointed on both ends and needing only shallow water. They came in a variety of sizes with large ones 66 feet long by six feet wide at

Dugout canoes were made by Native Americans of pine, black walnut, butternut or basswood from a hollowed out half log, shaped to a point on each end. Stone tools, shells and fire were used to form them. A well made dugout canoe was light enough to be portaged by one man. They were normally used for short trips and most often by women.

This is an image of an elm bark canoe similar to what was used by the Iroquois in New York. A frame was generally made of cedar pieces bound together with cedar or tamarack roots and then covered with a huge piece of elm bark. The ends of the bark were sewn together with cedar roots that had been scraped, split and soaked in water to make them pliable. The joints were sealed with a mixture of cedar and pine gum mixed with pitch. This type of canoe could be made quickly and, if destroyed on rapids, could be replaced relatively easily.

A packet boat on the Erie Canal. Quarters for passengers were below deck but on a pleasant day it was much more enjoyable to be on top and enjoy the scenery. However, bridges were numerous and low so very often the boatman yelled "low bridge" or blew a horn warning the passengers to lie down or go below deck.

the center and three feet deep, drawing only about 20 inches of water. On either side was a plank for men to walk on when poling the boat and there were seats for rowers. It often carried a square sail to take advantage of favorable winds. It carried drag ropes for use when the shoreline permitted men to walk along the water's bank and pull the boat upstream. The poles were used to push the boat upstream in shallow water where the ropes or oars could not be used.

The Durham was the type of boat that General George Washington used to move his soldiers across the Delaware River on December 25,1776 to capture the Hessian troops at Trenton, NJ. Boats of this style were sometimes referred to as Keelboats, Mohawks or Schenectady boats. There was likely some adaptation in size or style that gave the boat a name associated with the location in which it was made or used.

ERIE CANAL BOATS

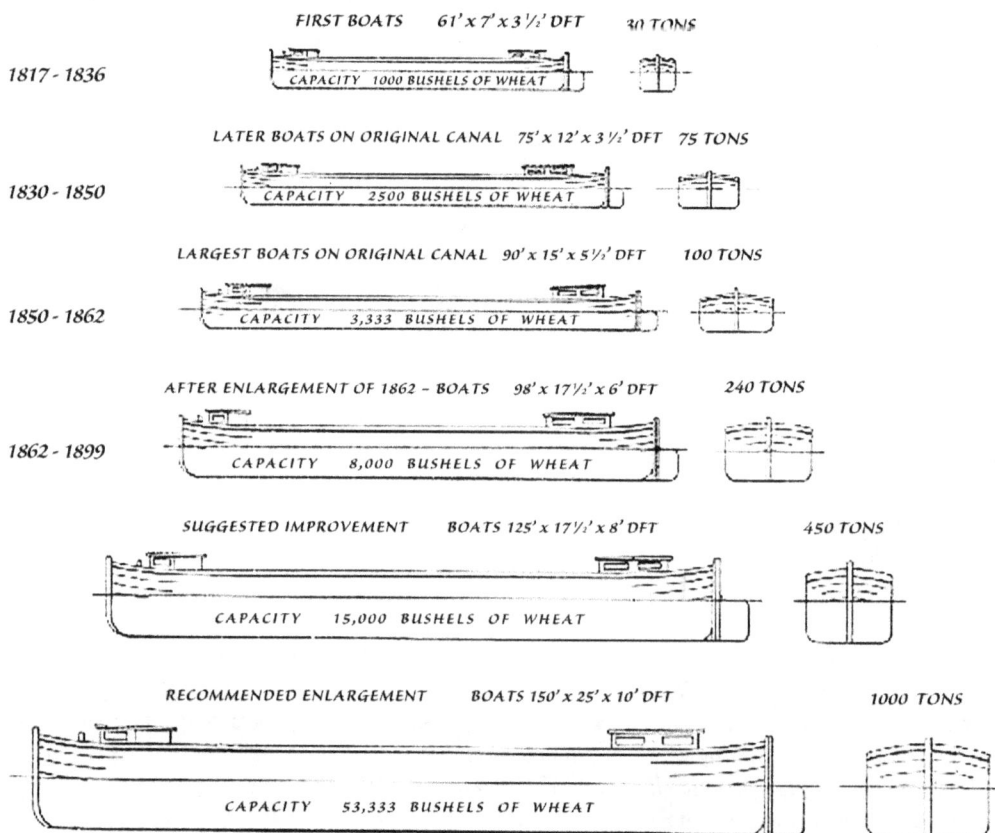

FIRST BOATS   61' x 7' x 3 ½' DFT   30 TONS
1817 - 1836   CAPACITY   1000 BUSHELS OF WHEAT

LATER BOATS ON ORIGINAL CANAL   75' x 12' x 3 ½' DFT   75 TONS
1830 - 1850   CAPACITY   2500 BUSHELS OF WHEAT

LARGEST BOATS ON ORIGINAL CANAL   90' x 15' x 5 ½' DFT   100 TONS
1850 - 1862   CAPACITY   3,333 BUSHELS OF WHEAT

AFTER ENLARGEMENT OF 1862 - BOATS   98' x 17½' x 6' DFT   240 TONS
1862 - 1899   CAPACITY   8,000 BUSHELS OF WHEAT

SUGGESTED IMPROVEMENT   BOATS 125' x 17½' x 8' DFT   450 TONS
CAPACITY   15,000 BUSHELS OF WHEAT

RECOMMENDED ENLARGEMENT   BOATS 150' x 25' x 10' DFT   1000 TONS
CAPACITY   53,333 BUSHELS OF WHEAT

A drawing showing how the size of the boats on the Erie Canal increased over the years. When the canal opened boats were designed to carry 1,000 bushels of wheat, which weighed 30 tons. When the canal was widened and deepened in the 1840s, boats carried 75 tons and after 1862 boats had a capacity of 240 tons, which was eight times the earlier boats' capacity. Courtesy of Erie Canal.org

An engraving of Robert Fulton's steamboat, 'Clermont', which successfully operated between New York City and Albany in 1807. The Clermont ushered in a new age of water transportation. Photo courtesy of New York State Archives.

Circa 1900 photograph of the 'Walter McMullin' which was constructed in Baldwinsville in 1887. This was prior to the trolley and automobile when travel by boat on our canals was common.

With the opening of the Erie Canal, packet boats for passengers and line boats for freight came into use. Packet boats were 60 to 90 feet long by just over 14 feet wide. They carried up to 60 passengers and consisted of a multipurpose room, which served as a lounge, dining room and sleeping room, and a kitchen. When the multipurpose room was used as a sleeping room a curtain was used to separate the ladies and the men. The average charge was four cents a mile, which included meals and sleeping accommodations. Passengers sat on the flat roof of the boat in good weather but had to be ready to lay flat when the call came out, "Low Bridge." Since the boat was pulled by horses or mules four miles an hour was a good pace of travel.[1] The packet boats had a regular schedule and often carried mail and freight besides passengers.

Freight boats, also called line boats, were usually family owned and had three sections. There was a large middle section for the freight, a small section in the bow for horses that were on break from towpath duties and another small section in the stern where the boat operator and his family lived. As the canals were widened and deepened and the locks enlarged, the size of the boats was increased so they could hold larger

loads. Continual use of the wooden boats and rotting of the wood shortened the life of many boats and in the later years of the Erie Canal boats made of steel began to come into use.

In 1807, Robert Fulton opened an era of successful transportation by steamboats on the Hudson River from New York to Albany. Steamships became quite common on the Hudson by the opening of the Erie Canal in 1825 but were experimental and of little consequence on canals until after they were widened, deepened and outfitted with larger locks. The 1880 Census reported that out of a total of 4349 canal boats 70 were steamers. Surprisingly, the steamers' average capacity was 140 tons while the traditional canal boats had average capacity of 172 tons.[2]

A.J. Christopher in an August 6,1964 article in the *Baldwinsville Messenger* suggests that Stephen Baldwin had a small steamboat that traveled from Baldwinsville to Oneida Lake in the early 1820s. This was before there was a canal between the two points and probably when the water level was high. The article also stated that Baldwin did run a steamboat between Baldwinsville and Syracuse making him the first to establish a merchant marine line between the two places.

1   Sadowski, Frank E. Jr. *The Erie Canal - Boats on the Erie Canal* p.1

2   Nostrant, Robert F. *Steam Canal Boats on the Erie Canal* p.2-6

Brown Boat Works at the foot of North St. in Baldwinsville. Several large excursion boats that plied the canals and lakes of New York were produced in this boatyard.

The launching of a U.S. Army lighter on the north end of Meadow Street by the Inland Waterways Equipment and Dredging Co. on June 4, 1918. The company had built dredging boats on the site for its use in building the Barge Canal and secured a contract to build 30 lighters for the government.

Quite a few steamboats are listed in the State register of steamboats that were involved in canal trade. Two of the earliest boats with a local interest were registered in 1849. Each had a capacity of 75 tons and were owned by Oneida L. & R. Steamboat Co., with a homeport of Oneida Lake. A steamship with its homeport at Phoenix had a registry of 1858. In Baldwinsville, the Jacob Amos, Jr., with a registry of 1874, was a passenger river packet of 20 tons and owned by Seth Brown. The Walter McMullin, built in Baldwinsville in 1887 with a registry of 1889, is shown as a Seneca River packet boat. The E.W. Tucker was a freight boat built in Phoenix with a homeport of Baldwinsville and was last listed in 1917. Several boats listed in the registry that were built in Baldwinsville with other home ports were the Wm B. Kirk, 93 tons and 92 feet long, built in 1887, and believed to be the last steamer operating on any old Erie Canal section (1919 in Rochester); the M.P. Brown, a passenger boat built in 1890 weighing 60 tons and

measuring 80 feet long; and the C.H. Francis, a freight boat built in 1895, 116 tons and 93 feet long.[3]

Shipyards appeared along waterways in many New York villages in the 1800s, including Fulton, Phoenix, Liverpool, Jordan and Baldwinsville. M.P. Brown operated two shipyards in Baldwinsville in the late 1880s and 90s. One was at the foot of North St. and the other was at the foot of Lock St. Brown made packet boats for both passenger and freight use that were powered by steam engines. Morris Machine Works manufactured engines for most of his boats. The boats averaged about 90 feet long by 18 feet wide and could carry between 250 and 500 passengers. Brown was also involved in packet boat navigation, operating a line of boats on Onondaga Lake that transported people to and from the numerous summer resorts along the lake.[4]

3   Nostrant, Robert F. *Steam Canal Boats on the Erie Canal* p.7-20
4   Christopher, A.J. *The Baldwinsville Messenger* February 1, 1968

The *"Melvin P. Brown"* of the Onondaga Transportation Line, on the Baldwin Canal in front of Morris Machine Works, loaded with passengers headed for a day of pleasure at a resort on Onondaga Lake.

The *"Busy Bee"* was a ferry boat located at King Ferry on Cayuga Lake. It carried wagons and passengers across the lake eliminating the necessity of an extra 50 miles to travel around the end of the lake. Originally it had a paddlewheel operated by a horse on a treadmill to power it the two miles across the lake, when the wind did not cooperate. Later a small steam boiler replaced the horse. It made its last trip in 1914 when the automobile eliminated the need of the ferry boat. Ferry boats were quite common in Central New York as a means of crossing lakes and rivers during the 1800s. Photo and information courtesy of Richard Palmer.

In an August 1,1963 article in the *Baldwinsville Messenger*, A.J. Christopher relates some freight costs by packet boat in 1895 as follows; three dump wagons shipped from Canastota to Syracuse, $3, one buggy from Lyons to Baldwinsville, 95 cents and a bundle of buggy whips from Rochester to Baldwinsville, 20 cents. This was before the day of shipping by truck and freight on the railroad would have been more expensive because of the small size of the shipments. The shipments by steamboat were not door-to-door like today's United Parcel Service but certainly filled the need that existed at that time.

The E.W. Tucker, which was a packet boat that hauled freight, was the last of the local steamboats and it hauled freight between Baldwinsville and Syracuse into the early 1920s leaving Baldwinsville about 9:00

The "Anna Lee," a private boat cruising on the Seneca in the early 1900s.

and returning at 4:30. It occasionally carried passengers but its principal cargo was merchandise for stores, including barrels of beer, coal, feed, farm machinery and raw materials as well as finished goods for Morris Machine Works and Penn Spring Works. At one time the boat was owned by Albert Perkins and Ernie Petley who had a dock along the Baldwin Canal at 18 E. Genesee St. and a barn for horses and wagons, to haul the freight, at the corner of Lock and Margaret Streets. Competition from the trolley express and from trucks diminished business on the canal and ended the days of the freight boat.[5]

There were also beginning to be steamboats designed for pleasure on the Seneca River beginning about 1880. They were much smaller than the commercial boats and were owned by a few of the wealthier families. Some of their names were Idlewild, Bess, Mable M., Dash and Gladys. They usually had an awning to provide shade from the sun and a coal-fired boiler which belched smoke and spewed ashes. They were about 20 to 30 feet

long and carried up to 10 passengers.[6]

Although they were never produced in large numbers there were at least two small pleasure boat manufacturers in Baldwinsville around 1900. In 1888, the New Process Rawhide Co. (later it moved to Syracuse and became known as New Process Gear) came to Baldwinsville and made rawhide canoes before turning to rawhide gears. In 1910, as recorded in Robert Nostrant's history notes, the Valley Boat and Engine Co. was located on Canton St. and sold both erected and knock-down frames for motor boats.

Improvements in the internal combustion engine brought gradual conversion of coal-fired steam boilers in both commercial and pleasure boats on the river. Numerous boat clubs were formed in Baldwinsville with the Sagawatha and Vagabondia becoming the most active ones with over 200 members. These clubs had boathouses, which were located above the dam, along the river and west of North St. Man's fascination

5 Christopher, A.J. *The Baldwinsville Messenger* Last of the Steamboats, August 8,1963

6 Christopher, A.J. *The Baldwinsville Messenger* Family Steamboat a Pleasure Craft, March 16, 1967

with speed appeared locally when a naphtha powered launch over 38 feet long, owned by several members of the Vagabondia Boat Club, appeared on the river in 1905. This sleek, speedy craft won many races on Upstate New York's waterways for a number of years.[7]

Transportation on our beautiful Seneca River, along its winding way across the fertile lands of central New York, has gradually changed from canoe, to bateau,

to Durham, to packet boats pulled by horses on the towpaths, to steamboats and finally boats powered by the internal combustion engine. Baldwin's dam was the first step in taming the Seneca, with the Barge Canal a century later finishing the task and turning the river into a smooth path for a pleasurable ride in a motorboat. It is difficult for today's observer to comprehend the changes that have occurred in the river, some for the better and, undoubtedly, some for the worse. Change is inevitable and there has been much, in only a few generations.

---

7   Christopher, A.J. *The Baldwinsville Messenger* Rise of Motor Boating in the Village, March 25,1971

The Vagabondia boat club boat house near the foot of North Street along the Seneca River. Boat clubs were popular in Baldwinsville in the early 1900s and the Vagabondia had over 100 members. You will note that one of the boat slips has the name 'Nokomis' at the top. The building still sits just west of Mercer Park.

A postcard titled 'Canoeing on the Seneca,' Baldwinsville, New York. The picture was likely taken in the early 1900s west of the dam. Canoeing was a popular recreational pastime on the Seneca in Baldwinsville for many years.

The Vagabondia and the Anna Lee on the Seneca River in Baldwinsville during the early 1900s. Both boat clubs and private motorboats were popular for recreation on the Seneca.

Our waterways provided an opportunity for winter fun as shown by this ice boat on Onondaga Lake. Ice boat racing was enjoyed on many lakes in Central New York, including Cross Lake, during the early 1900s.

Boats passing through Lock 24 of the Barge Canal in more recent times. Although the Barge Canal was constructed for large barges transporting freight, during the latter 1900s it became used almost completely by pleasure craft.

CHAPTER 13
Railroads

Who could have possibly envisioned a connection between the Revolutionary War battle of Bunker Hill and the first railroad in America? As the fiftieth anniversary of the Battle of Bunker Hill approached, a desire developed for a celebration of that bravely fought battle that led to the formation of the United States and the tremendous progress the country had made in the succeeding 50 years. It was decided to build what became the Bunker Hill Monument, an Egyptian style obelisk 221 feet high that could be seen for miles.

Plans were discussed and concern arose regarding the difficulty of hauling the monument's huge granite blocks three miles from the stone quarry in Quincy, Massachusetts to the Neponset River where they could be floated to the monument site at Charlestown. It was proposed that a special road be constructed that would hold up under the many heavy loads to be transported. It was decided to solve the problem by building a road of rails, later referred to as a "rail-road." This railroad opened October 7, 1826. The foundation for the road was of crushed granite that was topped every eight feet

with large flat stone sleepers. Two wooden pine rails twelve inches high and six inches thick were placed on the sleepers, five feet apart, with strips of iron three inches wide and one-quarter inch thick spiked to the top. Four railroad cars were made with both body and wheels made of wood. The wheels were six and one-half feet in diameter.

The October 9, 1826 *Boston Daily Advertiser* printed the following account of the opening of the railroad.

"This rail-road, the first we believe in this country, was opened on Saturday in the presence of a number of gentlemen who take an interest in the experiment. A quantity of stone weighing sixteen tons, taken from the ledge belonging to the Bunker Hill Association, and loaded on three wagons (railroad cars), which together weighed five tons, making a load of 21 tons, was moved with ease, by a single horse, from the quarry to the landing above Neponset Bridge, a distance of more than three miles.

E. L. Henry's portrayal of the Mohawk & Hudson Railroad during its inaugural trip between Albany and Schenectady in July 1831. The railroad now began to compete with the stagecoach for passenger traffic from the much slower Erie Canal with multiple locks between Albany and Schenectady. It was the beginning of the end of the stagecoach era. Courtesy of Richard Palmer

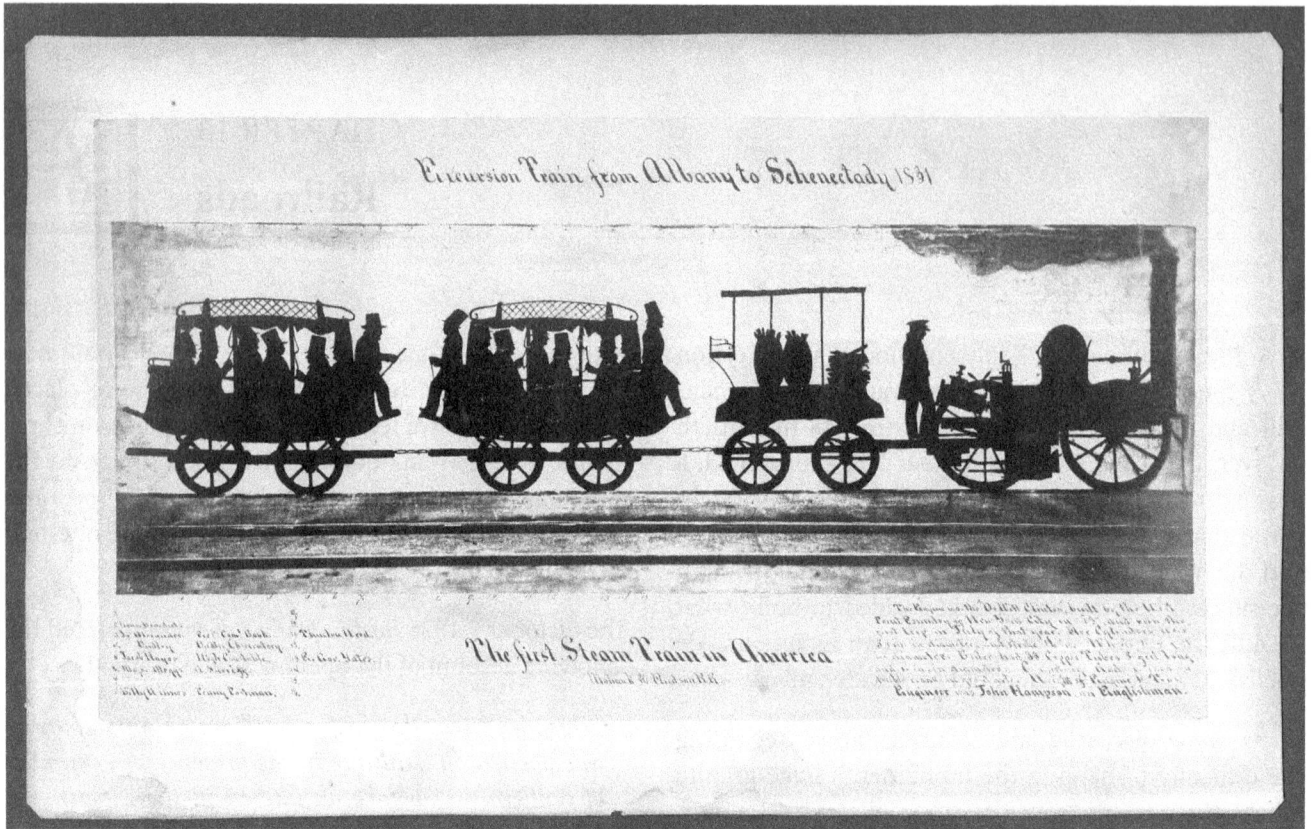

The first steam train in America traveled between Albany and Schenectady in July 1831. The engine was made by the West Point Foundry and the railroad was known as the Mohawk and Hudson. It traveled from Albany, where the Hudson River was navigable, to Schenectady where the Mohawk River was navigable. The railroad cars were converted stagecoaches. Courtesy of Albany Institute of History & Art

This road declines gradually the whole way, from the quarry to the landing, but so slightly that the horse conveyed back the empty wagons, making a load of five tons. After the starting of the load, which required some exertion, the horse moved with ease in a fast walk. It may therefore be easily conceived how greatly transportation of heavy loads is facilitated by means of this road."

The road held up well, the monument was completed 16 years later, and the railroad was powered by a horse all of those years.[1]

The Erie Canal had been completed in 1825 providing a convenient means for passengers and freight to travel from Albany to Buffalo. There was a substantial increase in elevation between Albany and Schenectady, requiring several locks, which made the approximately 17 mile trip exceedingly slow for canal passengers. Because of

this, Erie Canal passengers often traveled by wagon or stagecoach for this portion of the trip. Some investors recognized the opportunity for a railroad between Albany and Schenectady and in 1826 a charter was granted by the legislature to the Mohawk and Hudson River Railroad. On August 9,1831 it became the first railroad in New York State to haul passengers with a steam engine. This was only 11 years after the world's first public railroad had been planned in England. The engine, named the DeWitt Clinton after New York's seventh governor, was only 12 feet 10 inches long and weighed 6,758 pounds, about a fortieth of the weight of today's railroad locomotives. In Albany the train was pulled up State St. hill by cable because the engine lacked sufficient power. The cars seated 18 people and were similar to stagecoaches with three seats on the inside and one outside. The engine burned wood and belched smoke and sparks, which ignited passengers' clothing and parasols, as it traveled at 16 miles an hour across the countryside. Half way to Schenectady the train, with its cars chained together, stopped to take

1   Langdon, William Chauncy *Everyday Things in American Life 1776-1876*, p.329-334

106

on water, throwing passengers from their seats as each car was stopped by bumping against the next. (A train passenger suggested that a nearby wooden fence rail be fitted between the cars to help solve the problem.) The train continued to Schenectady where it was met with the music of bands, the roar of cannon and a large crowd of people.[2]

As we look back upon this event, seemingly insignificant to us today, it was one of the more important events in both New York's and Onondaga County's history.

_____

2 Palmer, Miss L. Pearl *Historical Review of the Town of Lysander* Part 111

This little 17 mile railroad was the beginning of the New York Central Railroad, which in 1853 connected New York City with Chicago and with other railroads eventually reaching to the Pacific Ocean. The Mohawk & Hudson's success spawned dozens of other railroads throughout the State, bringing with them significant business and growth. During the 11 years following the opening of the Mohawk & Hudson Railroad, eight other railroads were founded, each operating a segment between Schenectady and Buffalo. Initially these railroads were not built to compete with the Erie Canal's freight-shipping role and if freight was carried the railroads were required to pay the canal for any lost

An 1881 New York State engineer's map showing the major railroads and canals in Central New York. By this time the railroads offered service to a much greater proportion of people and businesses than the canals.

revenue. Eventually the railroads were allowed to carry freight during the winter when the canal was frozen, and later the legislature allowed them to compete during the entire year. By 1842, a person could cross the State by railroad but needed to change trains 10 times and buy a new ticket at each stop. In 1853, the railroads between Albany and Buffalo merged to form the New York Central. This merger increased railroad efficiency and gradually took business away from the Erie Canal. Two of the railroad companies that were part of the merger were the Syracuse and Utica and the Syracuse and Auburn, both powered by steam engines in 1839.[3]

On May 1, 1834 an act of the State legislature incorporated the Auburn and Syracuse Railroad with $400,000 of capital stock and on January 8, 1838 it opened between Geddes and Auburn. Stagecoach-like cars were pulled on wooden rails by Colonel John M. Sherwood's stagecoach horses. A year and a half later the first steam engine, appropriately named the Syracuse, was used to pull the cars on rails improved with a flat ribbon of iron on top, held down with spikes driven into the original wooden rails. Occasionally a spike would come loose, allowing an iron rail to pop through the coach floor. This loose rail was called a snake's head because of its curl similar to a snake.

By 1836, the legislature was besieged with petitions for railroads in all parts of the state due to the success of the first ones to be completed, and that year a charter was granted to the Syracuse and Utica Railroad. The following year two more area railroads were incorporated, the Syracuse and Onondaga to build a line from Syracuse to the stone quarries in the town of Onondaga, and the Brewerton and Syracuse Railroad Company.[4]

The Rochester & Syracuse Direct Railroad Company was formed in 1850, and in 1853 combined with the Auburn & Syracuse and the Auburn & Rochester to form the Rochester & Syracuse Railroad Company. This railroad bypassed Auburn, followed a more level route and was 22 miles shorter than the old line. It became part of the New York Central & Hudson Railroad during the consolidation of railroads in 1853.[5] This railroad passed through Warners and Memphis in the town of Van Buren.

In October of 1848 the 35 1/2 mile Syracuse and Oswego Railroad opened, nine years after the original survey had been made. It was profitable from the beginning. This railroad had depots in both Baldwinsville and Lamson and increased the opportunity of prosperity for people, farms and businesses along its route. Decline, however, came to communities some distance from the railroad as evidenced by Louis Dow Scisco's remark in the *History of Van Buren,* "After the building of the railroad to Oswego in 1848 the corners (Van Buren Center) relapsed into quiet that has never been aroused." In 1872, the Syracuse & Oswego Railroad became part of the Delaware, Lackawanna & Western.

October 1848, was also when the first train arrived in Baldwinsville. It was greeted with excitement by many of the local citizens. At that time, the railroad was not yet completed between Fulton and Oswego. The passengers disembarked at Fulton and were transported to Oswego by stagecoach. The railroad was originally of narrow gauge construction and when it was acquired by the D.L.& W. a third rail was added, making it possible for the existing trains as well as the D.L.&W. trains to use the tracks. Eventually the railroad became a standard two-rail system.[6]

Pearl Palmer in Part 112 of the *Historical Review of the Town of Lysander* provides an interesting picture of the Syracuse & Oswego Railroad at the Lamson station, about five miles north of Baldwinsville.

"Until about 1874 the engines of the Delaware, Lackawanna burned wood, and fuel houses were a necessity at intervals along the track. Two and one-half foot lengths of wood were stripped of bark (this given to the people) and stored for engine consumption. Likewise a spacious water tank must be located at short intervals. In Lamson the tank occupied a corner in the upper part of the fuel house which stood just north of the station. To raise water to the tank, from which it returned to the engine by gravity, required the operation of a hand pump, and for years the official pumper at Lamson was Harvey Butler. His morning exertions on the handle of a force pump provided a daily attraction for all the children in the community who stood about in silent awe to watch as the tank was filled for the thirsty engines, the water reaching them through a rubber hose."

3   Palmer, Miss L. Pearl *Historical Review of the Town of Lysander* Part 111
4   Bruce, Dwight H. *Onondaga's Centennial* p.227-230
5   Bruce, Dwight H. *Onondaga's Centennial* p.238-239
6   Hall, Edith *History of Baldwinsville* p.25, 39

A circa 1840 image of the Syracuse & Utica Railroad Co. terminal located in the center of the street between Salina and Warren St. in Syracuse. It was a small building with two tracks through the center and a waiting room that held 30 or 40 people. It was before the days of the telegraph and with only one track east and one track west a train couldn't leave the station until the one from the other direction arrived. The station was torn down in 1857. From a Forest to a City *by M.C. Hand*

WEST END OF THE OLD DEPOT.

The potato famine occurred in Ireland at the time of a great need for workers to construct the many railroads planned in New York. This brought a number of Irish to help in the construction of the Syracuse and Oswego Railroad. John Lamson built a tavern where the railroad tracks were to cross the Lysander-Phoenix highway and housed many of the laborers. Because the railroad passed several miles west of Phoenix, which didn't have a railroad until 1885, a large amount of freight traveled both ways between the railroad and Phoenix. In addition to freight, there was also considerable passenger traffic through the Lamson station with as much as $500 dollars in tickets sold in a single month. There were eight passenger trains, four in each direction, in addition to freight trains passing through Lamson and Baldwinsville each day. The passenger trains often took

their customers to intermediate stops where passengers boarded a train of another company, a steamboat, a packet boat or a stagecoach. An original timetable of 1850 noted that the morning train to Oswego connected to steamboats taking people to Sacketts Harbor, Ogdensburg, Lewiston, Rochester, Niagara Falls, Buffalo and Hamilton. The fare from Syracuse to Buffalo via railroad and steamboat, including board and berth on the steamboat, was $5.[7]

Merrick Smith Thompson of Little Utica was named boss of the railroad's construction in the Lamson area and upon its completion became station agent, a position he held until he retired in about 1884. He developed the

---

7   Palmer, Miss L. Pearl *Historical Review of the Town of Lysander* Part 112

The D.L. & W. Railroad passenger station in Baldwinsville circa 1910. It was located to the north of E. Genesee St. adjacent to the flour mill constructed by Frazee Milling Co. in 1923 at 75 E. Genesee St.

custom of keeping a daily diary of business transactions, weather reports and vital statistics. His daughter retained these records. Some of his comments, recorded between 1869 and 1879, are illuminating. He reported that the digging of potatoes was finished, people getting hurt, a case of smallpox, a drowning, balloon landing, Phoenix Fair, woodshed blown down, man killed by train, stranger died on train, Republican meeting, train wreck, election results, Lysander stage on runners, Tom Thumb and his wife went to B'ville and numerous other notations of the high points in life around Lamson. Of unusual interest was his sale of approximately 50 tickets at $7 each for an excursion train trip to the October 1876 United States Centennial celebration in Philadelphia. His reports regarding the weather often told of trains that were snowbound. One especially difficult time was in January 1879 when there was a five day railroad blockage caused by heavy snow. By the time the railroad was back in service, stranded passengers had consumed all the food and drink available in Lamson.[8]

Passenger service between Syracuse and Oswego was discontinued in 1949. People were now traveling by automobile or on the Syracuse and Oswego Motor Bus Line. Freight traffic on trucks also cut into the railroad's business. In 1960, the D.L. & W. merged with the Erie Railroad to become the Erie Lackawanna and 16 years later it was absorbed by Conrail.

Steam powered trains made their last trips on the D.L.& W. in 1951. Over a century of steam-powered locomotives passing through Baldwinsville and Lamson had come to an end. Steam whistles, soot and ashes disappeared with them. Charles Abbott, who grew up near the D.L. & W. in the 1940s, holds nostalgic memories of the steam powered trains. In the book *The Syracuse, Binghamton and New York Railroad* by the Central New York Chapter of the National Railway Historical Society, he relates some childhood experiences with trains in Baldwinsville.

"Dad sent eggs to New York City via the Railway Express Agency and many a time we would go to the passenger

---

8   Palmer, Miss L. Pearl *Historical Review of the Town of Lysander* Parts 113, 115, 116

station to drop the big wooden egg cartons and leave them on the baggage cart. Cars came in loaded with wheat for the International Mill, cellulose for the paper company, automobiles in boxcars for Van Wie Chevrolet, and coal for Tappan & Brooks and Waldron. Farmers loaded cars with cabbage and Morris Machine Works sent large pumps on flat cars. I spent a lot of time at the yard fascinated by both the trains and the workmen. One day a train workman told me to climb up into the engine cab. I looked in awe at the gauges, levers, pipes, valves, and the steam coming through the view windows on front. I was told to sit right there while the train crossed Oneida St. to hook on cars and not to climb down until they had connected the air."

There have been thousands of children and adults fascinated by steam powered trains passing through Baldwinsville and the surrounding area. Few had the experiences of Charles Abbott but most of us who saw those trains fondly remember them.

Syracuse & Baldwinsville Railroad

Baldwinsville, with a good supply of waterpower from its dam and the Baldwin Canal, connecting thru the Baldwinsville Canal to the Oswego and Erie Canals, had developed into a substantial manufacturing center. In 1880, there were five flour mills, a pump manufacturer, a sash and blind factory, a paper mill, a knitting mill and a number of tobacco warehouses. The canals could not be used in the winter, requiring road or railroad transportation several months each year. Roads were poor and not easily traveled in the winter. The Syracuse & Oswego Railroad (in 1872 it became part of the D.L. & W.) passed through the village in 1848 and was used by these manufacturing businesses but its tracks

A 1905 photo of a coal fired steam engine westbound train on E. Washington St. in front of the Syracuse City Hall. Syracuse was known across the United States as 'The City with Trains in the Streets'. In the 1920s there were an average of 90 train movements through the city each day, on streets filled with pedestrians, bicycles, wagons, horses and buggies. On September 24, 1936 the last train traveled at grade level across the streets of Syracuse. Photo courtesy of Richard F. Palmer

Syracuse & Baldwinsville train on bridge in Baldwinsville circa 1900. This bridge was located east of the present automobile bridge on Syracuse and Oswego Streets.

and freight station, located some distance from these businesses, required goods to be transported on wagons to and from the railroad, making extra handling and adding to the cost of shipping.

As early as 1874, an attempt had been made to have the D.L.& W. run a spur to provide the flour mills on the north side of Baldwinsville with convenient access to the railroad. Competition with larger flour mills in Western New York and beyond was fierce and the local mills needed to control costs in every possible way. They needed to have their carloads of wheat come directly to the doors of their mills and to be able to load their manufactured flour directly on railcars. The D.L. & W. refused their request for a rail extension, probably because of the cost versus the potential return available.

In 1881, the New York, Buffalo & West Shore Railroad was formed with stock of $40 million and opened in late 1883. It had a short life and went into foreclosure in 1885. It was sold at auction and was at once leased to the New York Central Railroad.[9] The West Shore paralleled the New York Central just south of the town of Van Buren. The competition between railroads that served similar markets was intense. Freight rates and passenger

fares sometimes dropped to almost nothing with only the stronger railroad surviving.

The West Shore created an opportunity for Baldwinsville's manufacturing interests, and on June 10,1886 an announcement was made of the formation of the Syracuse and Baldwinsville Railroad Company. $60,000 was raised from the sale of stock and $160,000 from first mortgage bonds at 6% for 50 years. Work started almost immediately, and property was purchased for the six mile, 66 foot right of way to the railroad station at Amboy. There was a vacant lot between the Amos and Frazee mills and between the Baldwin Canal and the river south of today's 16 E. Genesee St. that served as the Baldwinsville terminus. The terminal area was well below the level required to cross the river and because of its limited size, wooden trestles were constructed to reach the required elevation. The width of the river to be crossed was 350 feet requiring five piers and two abutments, which were constructed of limestone from the Union Springs quarry. A hill of gravel about three miles south of the village and near the railway was purchased. The gravel filled in the area near the trestles. About 100 Hungarian and Italian immigrants were employed to provide the labor force, and 50 teams of horses were hired to haul the various

9   Bruce, Dwight H. *Onondaga's Centennial* p. 259

materials. Amazingly, on November 30,1886 the first shipment was made on the railroad and it was officially opened on January 1. The following year a branch line of the railroad was extended in the middle of Water St., parallel to the race serving the manufacturers on the south side of the river in Van Buren.

There was no passenger service provided on the Syracuse and Baldwinsville Railroad until it had been operating for over a year. When passenger service commenced, the railroad offered four trains a day but only two provided close connections with the West Shore trains to Syracuse. Because of the need to change trains at Amboy and limited connections, the Syracuse and Baldwinsville Railroad did not give the D.L.& W. serious passenger competition. In an attempt to gain more passenger traffic they were very accommodating to

their customers, perhaps to the detriment of their freight business, consisting mostly of wheat, flour, feed and knit goods, which accounted for over 92% of the railroad's gross earnings in 1888. When the Baldwinsville Fair was in progress the railroad ran a train every 15 minutes and in September offered a special coach to the Syracuse Fair without a change of cars at Amboy. The railroad rented their passenger car, which was heated by stoves and had oil lights.[10]

The railroad transported 36,839 tons of freight in 1888, 72% of which was wheat to the flour mills and flour from the mills, along with pig iron and other metal products for Morris Machine Works. This was not enough to

10 Nostrant, Robert F. *The Syracuse and Baldwinsville Railroad* p.2-6

The D.L. & W. Railroad passenger station north of 75 E. Genesee St. with a coal fired engine approaching. On the right is the coal silo and elevator operated by Tappan & Brooks in the 1930s. A large proportion of homes and businesses in the Baldwinsville area used coal as a fuel from the late 1800s to the middle of the 1900s and depended upon the railroad to bring it to the area.

Looking east on Lamson Road at Lamson where the Syracuse & Oswego Railroad, now the D.L.& W., opened in 1848. The freight and passenger station is shown on the left.

make a profit as the railroad lost money during their fiscal year ending September 30 and was unable to meet its mortgage requirements. In early 1889, bond holders filed a foreclosure suit upon the railroad. Temporary financing permitted the continuation of operations, and on January 2,1891 the railroad was sold at auction to a representative of the original bondholders because there were no other bids. The railroad was reorganized as the Syracuse and Baldwinsville Railway Company and soon majority interest in the new company was purchased by the D.L. & W. The Syracuse and Baldwinsville Railway track was extended to connect with the D.L. & W. track on August 22,1891 and became known as the "New Branch." Passenger service to the Amboy station and freight service to West Shore Railroad were discontinued. During the foreclosure and sale of the Syracuse and Baldwinsville Railroad, information surfaced showing that the bonds investors purchased to finance the Syracuse and Baldwinsville Railroad had been represented as part of the Vanderbilt system and were guaranteed by the New York Central Railroad. This was false information to make the bonds salable. It is quite likely that the Syracuse and Baldwinsville Railroad would never have existed except for the dishonesty of an overzealous bond representative. The milling industry

in Baldwinsville was on the road of decline by 1887 as the centers of wheat production and the milling business both gradually moved further west, with more than one-half of the wheat production west of the Mississippi by 1877. Unquestionably, more wheat was turned into flour by Baldwinsville's mills than was produced in Onondaga County prior to the time of the construction of the Syracuse and Baldwinsville Railroad.

Although the railroad had discontinued passenger service from the old terminal of the Syracuse and Baldwinsville Railroad in 1892, the competition created by the arrival of passenger service on the Syracuse, Lakeside & Baldwinsville Railway to the north side of the river in 1900 again brought passenger service on the D.L. & W. back to the old terminal near the four-corners. The number of daily trains was increased, and a rate war developed allowing passengers to purchase a round-trip ticket to Syracuse or to the Onondaga Lake resorts for ten cents. In 1901, the two railway companies agreed to end the rate war, and D.L. & W. uptown service was discontinued.

There had been significant changes to several Baldwinsville manufacturing businesses between the construction of the Syracuse and Baldwinsville Railroad in 1887 and the beginning of Barge Canal construction in 1908. The Amos Mill and the Miller Knitting Mill had ceased operations. The Young Rake and Tool factory, the Kenyon Paper factory, New Process Gear and Hotaling Flour Mill had all been destroyed by fire. The construction of the Barge Canal put the icing on the cake since it was no longer practical to operate. The Syracuse and Baldwinsville Railway ended service to both the south and the north side mills. The railway bridge was dismantled during the next year.

The saga of the Baldwinsville and Syracuse Railway finally came to an end on January 24, 1944 when the State ordered that the company "is hereby dissolved." The only remaining assets to apply toward the over $150,000 owed to the D.L. & W. were 30.4 acres of the old right of way, which were sold for about $2,000. The more than 50 year history of the Syracuse and Baldwinsville Railroad, later becoming the Syracuse and Baldwinsville Railway had come to the end. These railroads were a significant part of Baldwinsville's transportation history and although never commercially successful, they affected the lives of many area residents.[11]

The trolley, an electric version of the railroad designed to carry passengers and light freight, is discussed in the next chapter.

_____

11 Nostrant, Robert F *The Syracuse and Baldwinsville Railroad* p.1-12 Note: The pages mentioned are from a reprint booklet prepared for the March 26, 1998 McHarrie Legacy meeting. Most of the material about the Syracuse and Baldwinsville Railroad and Railway came from the August 1995 volume of *The Green Block* while Mr. Nostrant was Town of Lysander Historian.

A Syracuse & Baldwinsville train traveling on the mill spur crossing Syracuse St., with the Baptist Church shown in the background. There is a snowplow on the front of the engine and the coal car attached on the rear.

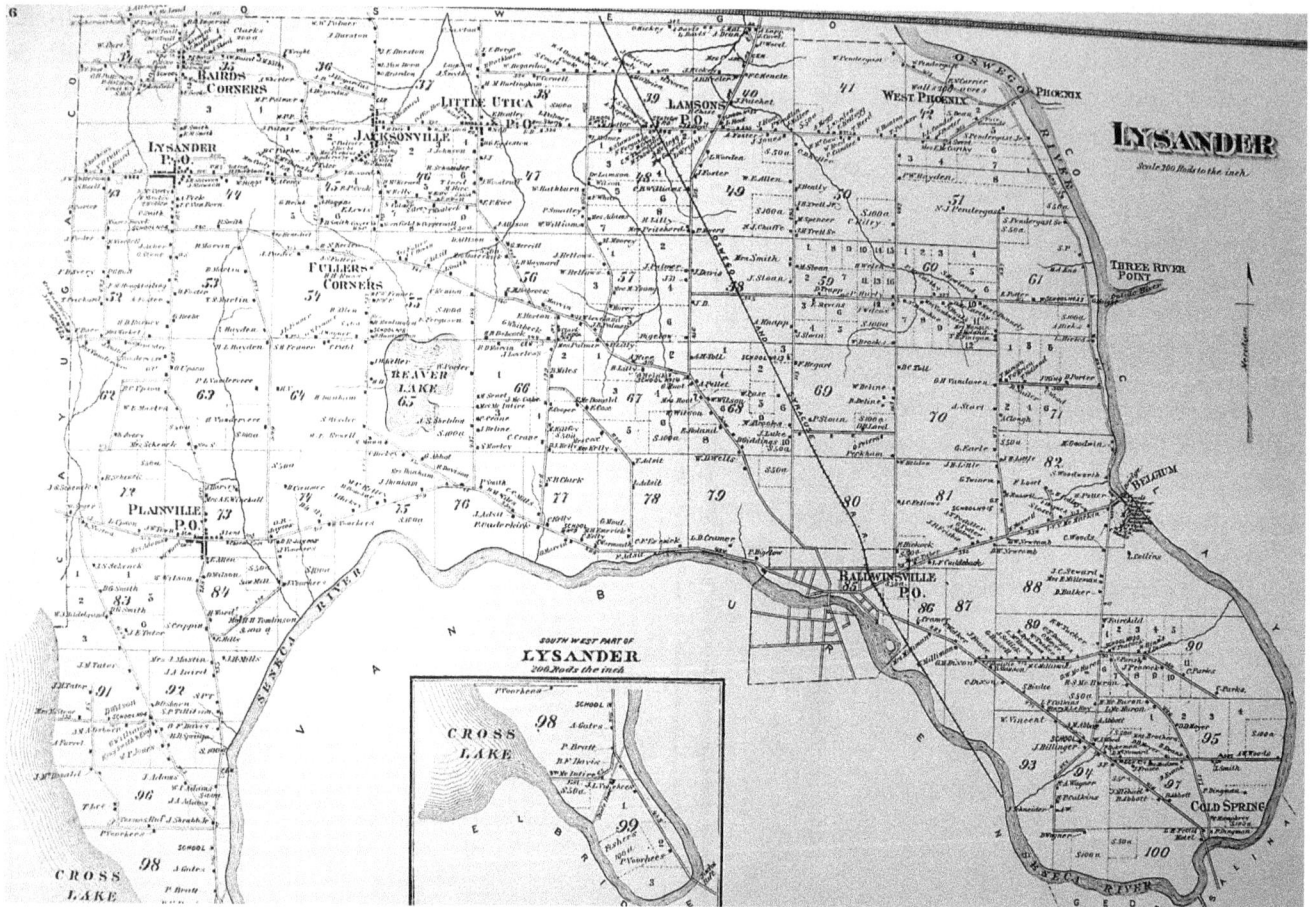

An 1874 map of the Town of Lysander by Homer D.L. Sweet that shows the path of the Oswego and Syracuse Railroad.

A photograph showing the Syracuse and Baldwinsville Railroad Terminal on the north side of the Seneca River. The Amos Mill is on the left and Morris Machine Works is in the background.

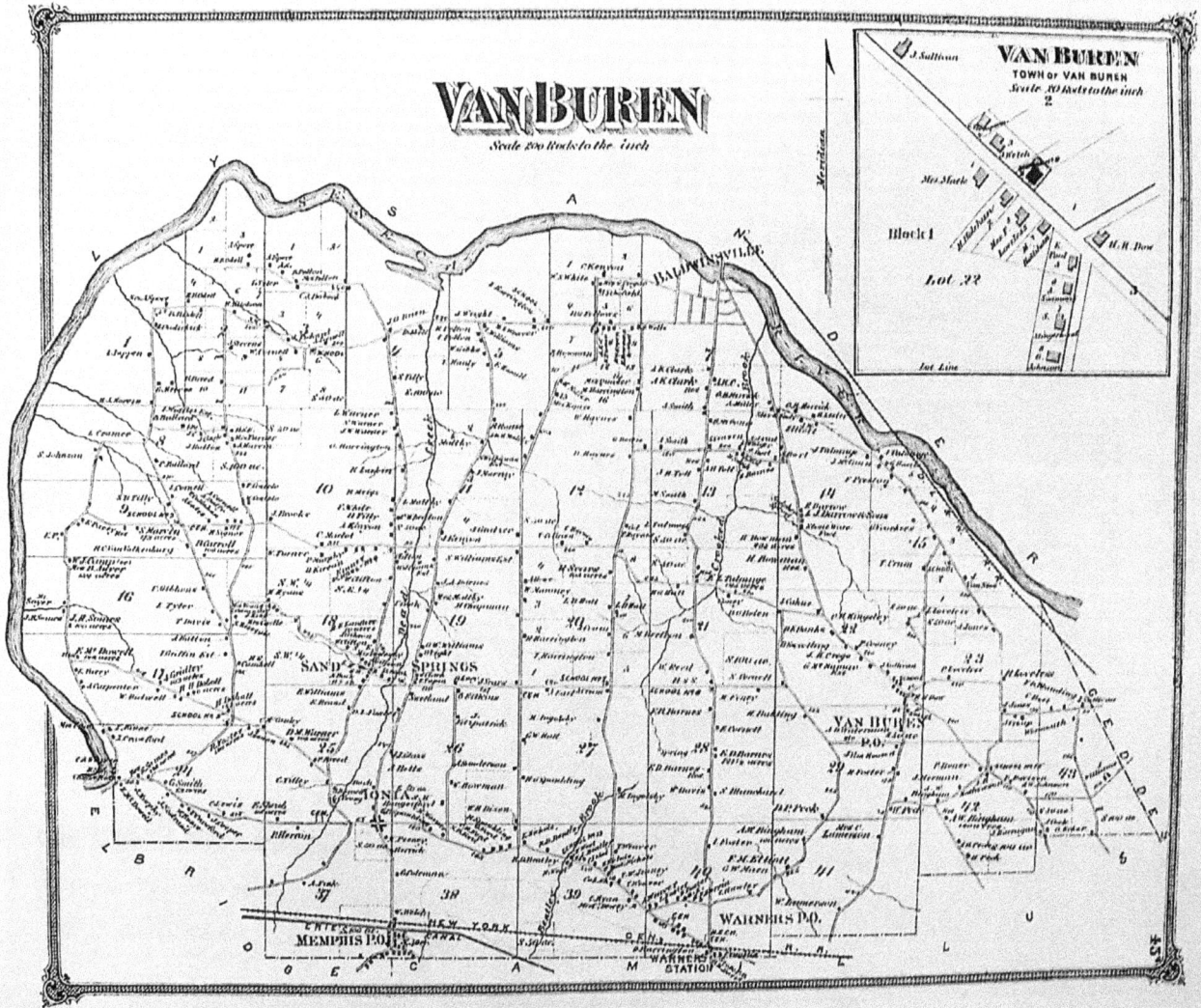

An 1874 map of the Town of Van Buren by Homer D.L. Sweet that shows the paths of the D.L. & W. Railroad along the Seneca River and the New York Central through Warners and Memphis.

CHAPTER 14

Horse-drawn and Electric Streetcars (Trolleys)

The names associated with street cars or trolley car are very confusing. Common terminology used in the Baldwinsville area was 'trolley' but other than early ones powered by horses, they were electric driven vehicles on rails powered by an electric current from an overhead wire. Usually they ran as a self-powered railway car while at other times, when customers were numerous, a second car without power was attached to the first. Company names sometimes included the word railway and at other times railroad but this chapter, whatever name is used, refers only to trolleys that were electric powered or their predecessors, powered by horses.

Although they never came to Baldwinsville, horse-drawn street cars played a significant role in city transportation. Street cars came to Syracuse in August 1860 with the first one operating between the Erie Canal Bridge at Salina St. and Wolf St. It was known as the Central City line. Gradually additional horse-car lines were built and by 1889 there were 12 separate lines. The last horse-drawn car to travel Syracuse streets was on October 1,1900. The end of the horse-drawn street car era began with the introduction of electric cars in 1888 when the Third Ward Railway electrified its line to Solvay. By 1890, through mergers and acquisitions, the numerous separate lines were merged under the People's Company or the Consolidated Company. In 1892, the Syracuse Street Railway Company purchased the two companies but legal difficulties held up the complete merger until 1895, and within a year it was sold to the Rapid Transit Railway Company.[1]

---

1 Galpin, W. Freeman *Central New York an Inland Empire,* *Volume II* p.129

Between 1860 and 1900 there were numerous horse drawn trolley companies that operated in various areas of Syracuse. Gradually a number merged; their demise began in 1888 with the introduction of electric trolleys. Photo courtesy of OHA Museum & Research Center.

A Syracuse, Lakeside & Baldwinsville Railway trolley at the west side of Onondaga Lake resort area in the early 1900s. The trolley has a big load as it is pulling the double-decker. On Sundays and holidays during the summer, people from Syracuse and Baldwinsville flocked to these summer resorts.

Double decker Syracuse, Lakeside & Baldwinsville trollies in downtown Syracuse heading toward Baldwinsville and perhaps leaving passengers at the New York State fairgrounds or at the Onondaga Lake resorts during the early 1900s. Photo courtesy of OHA Museum & Research Center.

The horse-drawn streetcars were a throwback to the very first railroads, quite similar to the one between Geddes and Auburn which opened in 1838. The streetcars were larger vehicles that held more people and were operated as single units. One can imagine the effort of the horses pulling these cars up some of the hills in Syracuse. There is no question that street routes were often chosen with an eye to location difficulty and hills. Most certainly there were times when the younger and stronger passengers exited the car and walked to ease the horses' burden on the steeper hills.

In 1900, the Rapid Transit Railway Company had control of 21 streetcar lines in Syracuse which covered 54 miles. By 1905, the streetcar lines covered 68 miles but five years later that number had dropped to 52 miles as the automobile began to be more common. A transfer system developed allowing passengers to travel from one part of the city to another for five cents. In the early 1900s, Rapid Transit became part of New York State Railways, and in 1936 Syracuse Transit Corp. took over the Syracuse branch of New York State Railways. At that time they were given permission to operate motor bus lines in Syracuse and by 1941 all the electric streetcars had left the city streets.[2]

The electric trolley cars that started in Syracuse gradually were extended to provide service in the direction of Baldwinsville when the Onondaga Lake Railway was chartered in 1896. It became the Syracuse, Lakeshore and Baldwinsville Railway (S.L.&B.) in December 1897 but a trolley did not reach Baldwinsville until September 24,1899. In 1898, it was originally a single track that carried people from Syracuse to Maple Bay and to resorts along the west side of Onondaga Lake. This was before the dumping of Solvay Process waste along the lake. The original equipment for the 18 mile line consisted of 14 motorcars, 12 trailers and several snowplows. Syracuse is actually only 12 miles from Baldwinsville but the additional miles came from tracks to the resorts and the railway following the winding highways to Baldwinsville.[3]

---

2   Galpin, W. Freeman *Central New York an Inland Empire, Volume II* p.129-131
3   Gordon, William R. and McFarlane, James R. *The Rochester, Syracuse and Eastern "Travelectric" 1906-1931* p.130

Trolley heading south across the Seneca River bridge in Baldwinsville. The bridge was constructed in 1900 and permission was granted by the towns of Van Buren and Lysander for the Syracuse, Lakeshore & Baldwinsville Railway to run its tracks across the new bridge. Miller knitting mill is the large building in the center and the Presbyterian Church steeple can be seen in the upper right. Circa 1901 by Gardner & Davis

Trolley heading south on Oswego Street after making the sharp curve from E. Genesee St. in Baldwinsville. The picture was taken after 1905 when Clifford D. Beebe purchased the railway, reorganized it, installed a double track and renamed it the Syracuse, Lakeshore and Northern. A new ticket office with waiting room was constructed at 10 E. Genesee St. in 1913. The spire of the Presbyterian Church is in the upper left.

Two new double deckers arrived in 1899 followed by seven more later. They were given the term '15 bench cars'. They had a double bench running the length of the car on the second deck, and could carry 100 people. During the summer, on a Sunday or a holiday when the weather was fine, people jammed the trolleys and some rode hanging on to the outside.

The company generated its own electricity at its powerhouse in Lakeland, adjacent to its car barn and just north of Nine Mile Creek, five miles from Syracuse. Originally just passenger service was offered but later express service, the shipping of small items, was added and totaled $356 in 1902. The same year the S.L.& B. sold 31,384 tickets and collected cash fares from 1,237,071 passengers. Because they were dependent for most of their business on the summer traffic to the Onondaga Lake resorts, they lost money and went into receivership in December 1903. Another reason for losing money was the number of free passes they gave away to obtain

rights of way from landowners and other favors. In 1905, Clifford D. Beebe purchased the railway, reorganized it and named it the Syracuse, Lakeshore and Northern Railroad.

The terminology used for the electric trolley system is very confusing. Common terminology was trolley but they were electric driven vehicles on rails powered by an electric current from an overhead wire.

Beebe was the owner of a number of electric railways and immediately started to improve the Syracuse, Lakeshore and Northern Railroad by installing a double track to Baldwinsville, improving the roadbed, removing many of the curves and making the railroad both shorter and faster. Traveling at speeds up to 60 miles an hour, a trip from Baldwinsville to Syracuse was now made in less than 30 minutes. Beebe also made plans to extend the railroad to Phoenix and Fulton, completing it to Fulton in 1909 and to Oswego in 1911. The line north of Baldwinsville was graded for double track but only one was ever laid. There were occasional turnouts for trains to meet and there was a short passing track between Phoenix and Fulton. When plans were made for the Barge Canal, the bridge over the Seneca River needed to be replaced and a double track bridge was constructed. A bridge was also built over the D.L. & W. tracks near the Stiles station. The span over the tracks was 141 feet long, with each approach over 300 feet long, making its total length over 800 feet.[4]

The first trolley line to Baldwinsville entered the village on the south side at Crooked Brook (near 108 Syracuse St.) and continued to the river at Water St. At that time there was no Barge Canal and the bridge over the river wasn't considered safe for trolleys to pass over. Tickets were sold at 12 Syracuse St. in a store owned by Bill Ellis. When a new bridge was constructed over the Seneca River in 1900, permission was granted for the trolley to run its tracks over the bridge. The tracks followed Oswego St. to East Genesee, then east to Palmer Lane (previously called Creamery Corners) and then north through what is now the Baldwinsville Central Schools property (near the bus garage) and on to Phoenix where it crossed the Oswego River. Small hexagon trolley

4   Gordon, William R. and McFarlane, James R. *The Rochester, Syracuse and Eastern "Travelectric" 1906-1931* p.130-131

stations were placed at key locations along the trolley track for patrons who were waiting for a trolley. A door was on one side with benches on the other five sides and there were electric heaters near the roof for cold weather comfort.[5]

When the trolley was able to cross the river and continue north, a trolley ticket and freight office was constructed between E. Genesee St. and the Baldwin Canal at the present 10 E. Genesee St. The building was completed in 1913. The ticket office with waiting room was in the front of the building, later becoming Lysander Town Offices. The freight office was in the rear, becoming the Baldwinsville Public Library at a later date. The author has pleasant memories, as a member of the Lysander Planning Board, meeting in the old trolley station. A timetable for 1912 showed a total of 66 daily runs to Baldwinsville, with 33 each way. This schedule offered fast, convenient service for both passengers and small freight shipments to Syracuse and points north.[6]

5   Connell, Ruth M. and Christopher, Eleanor T. *Baldwinsville Trolley Trivia* (Written for the Beauchamp Historical Society in 1985)

6   Connell, Ruth M. and Christopher, Eleanor T. *Baldwinsville Trolley Trivia* (Written for the Beauchamp Historical Society in 1985)

1904 image of a Syracuse, Lakeside & Baldwinsville electric car loaded with passengers. This railcar was moving rapidly (they could travel at speeds up to 60 miles an hour) with both men and women standing on the outside steps, hanging onto the car. They were likely heading to the resorts on the west side of Onondaga Lake. Photo courtesy of OHA Museum & Research Center.

February 1920 image of a Russell railroad plow and a passenger railway car just south of West Phoenix. The electric railway car lost power during a snow storm and when the power returned the car was snowed in and had to be shoveled out. Becoming stranded was not uncommon for either trolleys or railroad trains during the winter in the heavy snows north of Baldwinsville. Photo courtesy of OHA Museum & Research Center.

The lack of technology in the early 1900s, coupled with limited training of trolley operators and the significant number of trolleys passing through Baldwinsville each day, created circumstances where there were bound to be accidents. Besides relatively common accidents like a cow being hit, there were some that were really serious. In 1815, Thad Haynes had finished threshing grain for Isaac Hay on Ellsworth Road, and in the late evening moved his equipment to another farm on the other side of the trolley tracks. There were no street lights in the area he was crossing, which was near Crooked Brook and the current Evans Chevrolet. His lengthy steam engine and threshing machine almost made it across the tracks but the fast moving trolley did not have time to stop and caught the rear end of the threshing machine. Two men were instantly killed and a number of other people injured. The 90 degree turns at the Baldwinsville four-corners and at Creamery Corners became disastrous if brakes failed or some other portion of the equipment malfunctioned. At Creamery Corners, when brakes on

a trolley failed one day, the trolley went off the tracks, overturned and injured over twenty people. The local doctors came to their aid and a few were transported to the hospital at Syracuse. Another time the brakes failed on a special trolley, with just a motorman and conductor on board, as it approached the four-corners. Both were helpless but had the presence of mind to jump out before the trolley crashed and neither was hurt.[7]

Snow provided a great challenge for the trolleys, especially north of Baldwinsville toward Oswego. They had plows but they were often unable to keep up with the blowing and drifting snow. Sometimes when a trolley was stopped by a drift it was necessary to back up and come into the drift at great speed in an attempt to get through. One time when a trolley couldn't make it through a drift near Phoenix, it backed up nearly a mile

---

7   Connell, Ruth M. and Christopher, Eleanor T. *Baldwinsville Trolley Trivia* (Written for the Beauchamp Historical Society in 1985)

to gain speed and came hard into the drift. They almost made it but when they tried to back up again they found that the trolley wheels were about 100 feet back and the car body was resting on two feet of hard packed snow![8]

In 1912, a devastating tornado struck the summer resorts at Long Branch. Buildings, trolleys and people were tossed about by the devastating winds and several people were killed. The resort was rebuilt but business deteriorated afterwards and affected business for both the resort and the trolleys.

In 1914, the Syracuse, Lakeshore and Northern Railroad was merged with the Rochester, Syracuse and Eastern

to form the Empire United Railways, Inc., which in 1917 was sold at a foreclosure sale to the Empire State Railroad. In 1929, this company went into receivership. The era of trolley cars ended on June 24,1931 when the last car passed through Baldwinsville.[9] For over 30 years residents near Baldwinsville had been provided with convenient transportation to Syracuse. The internal combustion engine and pneumatic rubber tires had become the winners over the electric motor and rails. The convenience of travel from door to door without need for intermediary transportation was the ultimate winner.

8   Gordon, William R. and McFarlane, James R. *The Rochester, Syracuse and Eastern "Travelectric" 1906-1931* p.133

9   Gordon, William R. and McFarlane, James R. *The Rochester, Syracuse and Eastern "Travelectric" 1906-1931* p.130-133

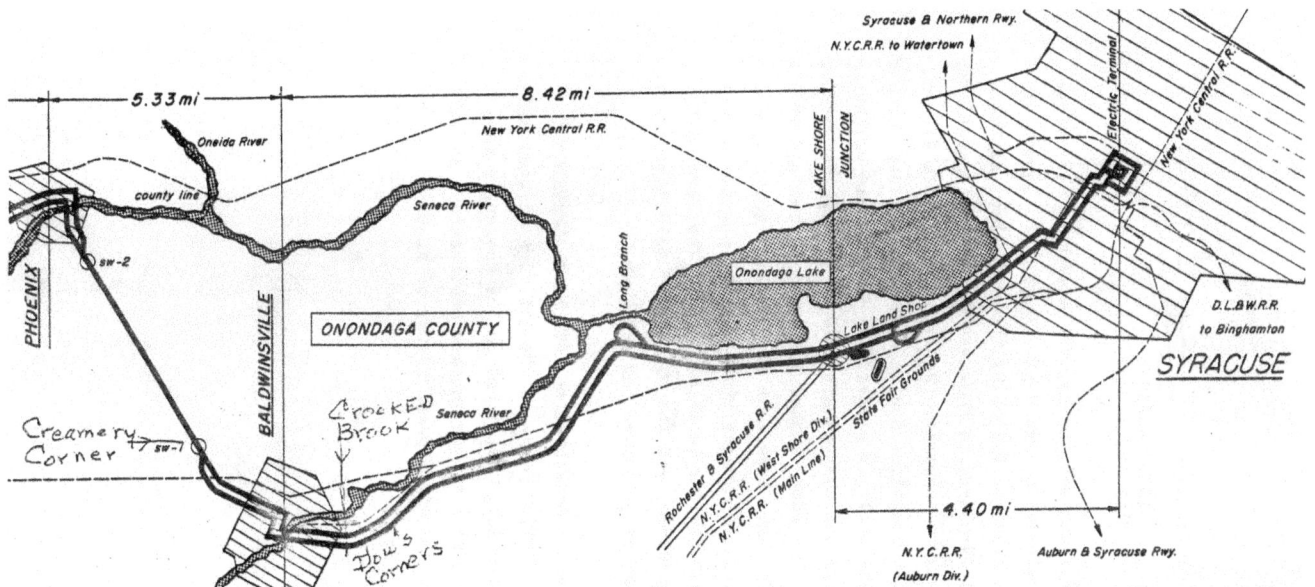

1923 map of the Empire State Railroad, which originated as the Syracuse, Lakeside & Baldwinsville Railway reaching Baldwinsville in 1899. At this time it was a double track system from Syracuse to approximately where the Baldwinsville Central Schools' bus garage is located. (The location of Creamery Corners is incorrect and was actually within the village of Baldwinsville at approximately 43 E. Genesee St.) Drawing is taken from Baldwinsville Trolley Trivia *by Ruth M. Connell and Eleanor T. Christopher.*

BALDWINSVILLE TROLLEY ROUTE

Crooked Brook Area

Mildred Ave.

Hotaling St.

Downer St.   Downer St.

Grove St.   Grove St.

                              Tappan St.

Water St.   Water St.

Barge Canal

Seneca River

Old Baldwin Canal

1st Ticket Off.

Trolley Ticket
Office and
Freight Station

East
Genesee St.   West Genesee St.

Creamery Corner

Albert Palmer Lane

Elizabeth St.

East Oneida St.   West Oneida St.

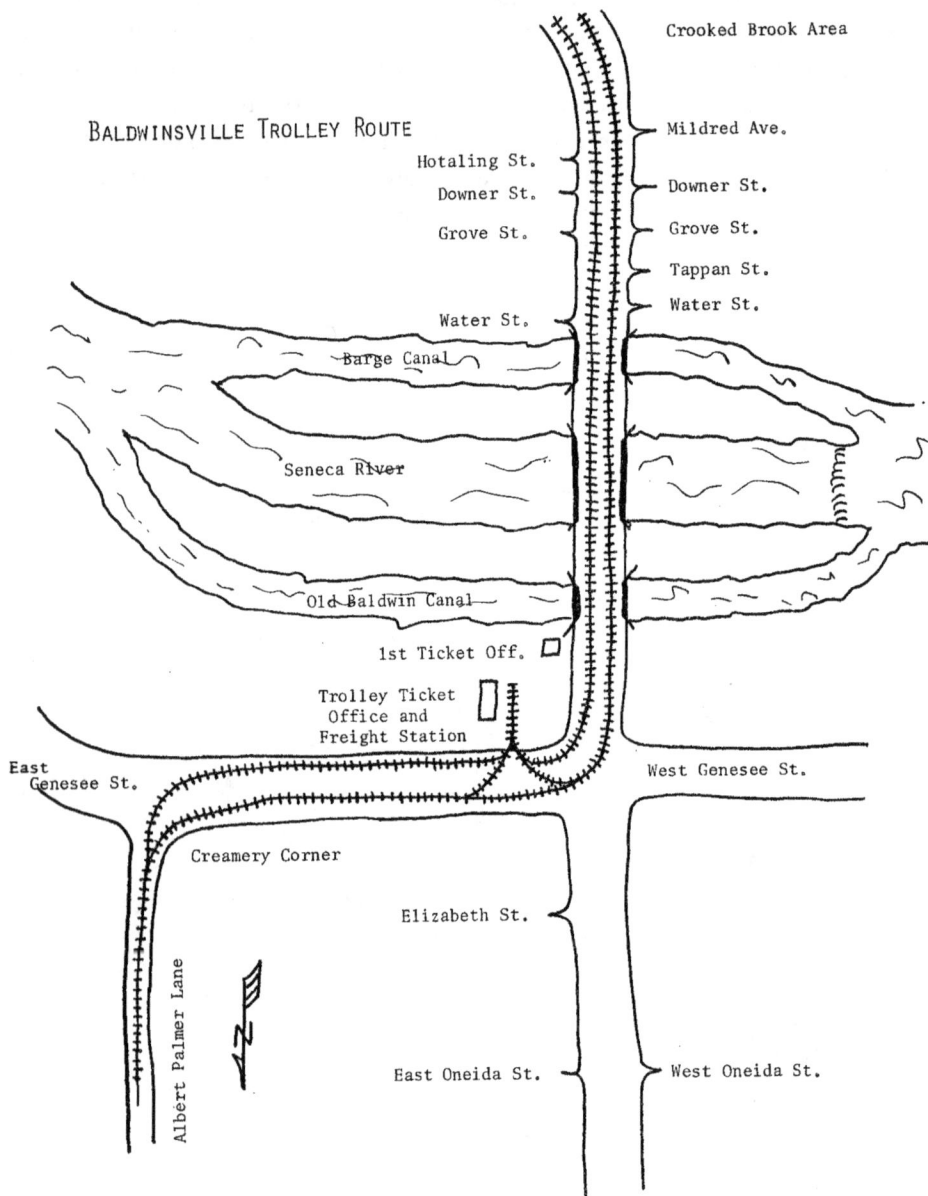

A map of the Baldwinsville trolley route including the location of the trolley ticket office and freight station at 10 E. Genesee St. where Key Bank is currently located. Notice the sharp turns at the Baldwinsville four-corners and at the intersection of E. Genesee and Palmer Lane. Numerous accidents occurred at these corners. Drawing is taken from Baldwinsville Trolley Trivia *by Ruth M. Connell and Eleanor T. Christopher with drawings by Rosina C. Ford.*

lthough airplanes were not a major player in transportation during the time period covered by this book, during the past century airplanes have become an essential part of almost everyone's life. Even if a person does not fly, many of the items he eats or uses on a daily basis are transported by airplanes. Airplanes appeared on the scene in the early 1900s and by the 1930s Syracuse area residents were flying in and out of the airport at Amboy. The author had the thrill of his first commercial airplane ride from the old Syracuse Airport at Amboy before its move to the Hancock Airport at Mattydale.

Air travel had its beginnings in Central New York, just south of Van Buren at Amboy in 1912 when Harry Atwood landed there on a flight from New York City to Chicago. By 1925, the little airport was a busy spot and chosen by Syracuse Mayor Charles Hanna to become the Syracuse Airport at Amboy. The airport was purchased for $50,000, was opened in 1927 and operated by the Syracuse Parks Department.[1] Airmail was first delivered to the airport in 1928 and by the 30s Ford Tri-motor planes were regularly landing on the airport's three grass runways.

There were a number of notable early aviators that landed at the airport including Charles Lindberg in the "Spirit of St. Louis" in 1927 with a crowd of 2,000 waiting to greet him. Other notables were Will Rogers and Wiley Post in 1931, General Jimmy Doolittle in 1932 and Amelia Earhart in 1936.[2]

During World War II, the airport became a flight training center. On December 31, 1941, the Air Force authorized the construction of an air base near Syracuse and purchased 3,500 acres, which became known as the Mattydale Bomber Base. B-24s were assembled

1   History About Syracuse Airport, *Syracuse Hancock International Airport* p.1
2   History of Town of Camillus, *Town of Camillus* p.2

An aerial photograph of the Syracuse Airport at Amboy taken in 1940. It served as Syracuse's airport until after World War II when Syracuse took over the Mattydale Bomber Base for use as an airport. Photo courtesy of OHA Museum & Research Center.

and tested at the Air Base to be sent to fly bombing missions from England. In 1946, Syracuse took over the Mattydale Bomber Base on an interim lease, and in 1948 it was dedicated as a commercial airfield. It was named the Clarence E. Hancock Airport and opened to the public in 1949.

The Amboy Airport continued to operate as an airfield for small private planes for a number of years and was eventually purchased by the Solvay Process Co. as a disposal site for waste sludge.

An image taken at the Syracuse Airport at Amboy in 1930. Notice the boxes that have shipped to Syracuse by airplane being loaded into the Dey Brothers & Co. department store truck. The airport had been been purchased and put into use by Syracuse in 1927. Photo courtesy of OHA Museum & Research Center.

A crowd at the Syracuse Airport at Amboy on August 18, 1938, greeting Douglas 'Wrong Way' Corrigan. A month earlier Corrigan had flown nonstop from Brooklyn to Ireland although he had filed a flight plan to go from Brooklyn to California. He claimed that he had misread his compass and due to clouds had flown in the wrong direction. Since previously his request to fly solo nonstop to Ireland had been denied, it looked suspiciously like it was deliberate. He was treated as a hero although he never admitted to doing it intentionally. Photo courtesy of OHA Museum & Research Center.

CHAPTER 16

A Reflection on the History of Transportation

Today, rapid and convenient transportation has become an important and expected aspect of our daily lives. We seldom give transportation a thought except when inconvenienced by an automobile breakdown or an act of nature disrupting our daily schedule.

Think back to our ancestors trudging through the wilderness to the Baldwinsville area. Ponder the poor immigrants digging the Baldwin and the Erie Canals by hand, hundreds dying because of malaria and other diseases. Give thought to the men cutting paths through the forest and making roads so others could travel a little easier. Think of the thousands of land owners each year paying their taxes by maintaining local roads. Remember the people who hauled thousands of tons of rocks to the stone crushers and mixed the concrete by hand to make our first concrete roads. We take all of these efforts and sacrifices along with hundreds of others not mentioned for granted as we go about our daily lives. Each day as we eat and use goods from all parts of the world, and as we move from point to point with ease, it is appropriate that we remember the efforts of millions of people who have made this possible through the tremendous innovations in transportation.

Human beings have existed on Earth for several hundred thousand years and almost all of that time have been totally dependent upon only their two legs to move themselves and their goods from one place to another. Historic records date back only a few thousand years so we have no idea when someone noted a tree floating in water and decided to jump on and go for a ride. Eventually, early man found that a certain size or kind of tree floated better than others and that a vine could be used to lash several small trees or branches together to make a raft. Rafts were used for thousands of years before it was discovered that trees could be hollowed through a process of burning and chipping with stone tools to form what we might call a boat.

Historical records of the last several thousand years show the gradual improvement in boats, from man powering them with poles and oars to the development of sails to capture the power of the wind. Human and wind power to move boats was all that was available until just a little over 200 years ago when the use of steam boilers began furnishing a dependable source of power for travel on water.

Archeological evidence suggests that cattle may have been domesticated approximately 14,000 years ago. Their domestication would have brought the development of the ox yoke permitting oxen to drag loads. Archeologists estimate that the first wheels may date to about 10,000 years ago but it would have taken many years before a cart with wheels was developed to carry people. Horses are estimated to have been domesticated in the area of what is now the Ukraine about 6-9,000 years ago. These horses were much smaller than the ones we have today and likely were first used to pull carts. As the size of horses increased they began to carry riders.

The United States is a young country, only 236 years old. At the time our country was established, there were sailing ships and stagecoaches but travel for the multitude of individuals continued to be by walking. Within the next 50 years steamships and canals began to come into use and a few years later railroads appeared. Roadways were cut through the forests making travel convenient for oxcart, wagon and stagecoach. Even with these advancements, transportation for the vast majority of people continued to be by walking well into the 1800s. Manufactured goods and food were both produced close to home and needed to be transported only short distances. In rural areas farmers lived where they worked and in villages most people walked to work. Horse streetcars began to appear in cities after the Civil War and electric street cars in the late 1800s.

With the appearance of canals and railroads production of food and manufactured goods began to move to the sections of the country where goods could be produced economically, and reach markets with a cost less than its competitors. As a result, production moved further and further from the points of consumption because of the availability of cheap and dependable transportation. As transportation continued to improve, production could move to any point on planet Earth.

The changes in production locations also had an effect upon the movement of people. With large production centers, people moved to those locations to fill the need for workers. This resulted in a movement of people from farms and villages to cities in the late 1800s and first half of the 1900s. Cities grew rapidly causing an increase in the need for trolleys to move workers short distances from home to work.

The invention and the common use of the internal combustion engine began to change the face of America by the 1920s. Highways were improved and people could easily travel 5, 10, or even 20 miles to attend an event, shop or work. Retail stores became larger and were located further apart. Manufacturing facilities increased in size. A large proportion of the population could now jump into an automobile and be wherever they wanted in a matter of minutes.

Between the Great Depression and the end of World War II there was limited change in the transportation of goods and people. Beginning in 1946, there was an explosion in transportation throughout the United States. Automobiles and trucks were sold as rapidly as they could be produced, and airline travel ballooned. Returning veterans married, started families and moved from the cities to suburbia. Schools consolidated and many students who had previously walked rode the bus to school. Air conditioning made summer living in the South comfortable and winter living there desirable. Factories moved, people moved, and manufactured goods and food moved along with them.

World War II demonstrated that the United States was now the number one world power and it continued to make the same statement after the war with its international presence. America sold its products in almost all corners of the world and its companies began to manufacture goods and to have retail stores in many countries. Airplanes made any part of the world closer, in time of travel, than to go just from Albany to Buffalo 200 years earlier.

As time progressed through the late 1900s and into the 21st century, the extent of transportation use continued to expand. Huge ships holding hundreds and then thousands of tractor-trailer size containers were built. Airplanes became both larger and faster, further shrinking the size of the planet. Huge pipelines were constructed to move petroleum products, tractor trailers became larger and a new interstate road system brought all sections of the country closer to each other. America, its raw materials and its manufactured goods were on the move!

The US government tells us there are over 250 million registered motor vehicles in the US today and that airlines transport over 500 million passengers in the US each year. Add to those numbers the people moving on buses, boats and trains! America is a country whose people rely heavily upon our transportation system.

Transportation, beyond our planet, expanded to the moon when astronauts landed and returned safely in 1969. A space station was developed with astronauts inhabiting it months at a time. Bathyspheres and the bathyscaphe were developed to permit man to descend and explore into the depths of the oceans. Man continued to develop improved and new means of transportation that brought information previously unknown.

A person can only wonder what new forms of transportation may be developed in the future. Perhaps our moon will be the next spot we colonize. Will we travel to Mars or a moon on Jupiter and establish settlements there? Will man travel through space to different planets through worm holes at speeds faster than light?

Two hundred years or even a hundred years ago, no one could have imagined the tremendous changes that have occurred in transportation. Similarly, no one today can foresee what will develop in the next 200 years. It would be worthwhile for each of us, however, to take a few moments to marvel at the changes in transportation that have taken place since our country was founded and even during our own lifetimes. The diversity and extent of these changes are hard to comprehend!

Bibliography

Albany Gazette

Baldwinsville Messenger

Beauchamp, William M., *Past and Present of Syracuse and Onondaga County, New York, from prehistoric times to the beginning of 1908* (New York: S.J. Clarke Publishing Co., 1908).

Belknap, Jeremy, *Dr. Belknap Tour to Oneida 1796*

Bellamy, James F., *Cars Made in Upstate New York* (Red Creek, NY, Squire Hill Publishing Company, 1989)

Boston Daily Advertiser

Bruce, Dwight H., *Onondaga's Centennial: Gleanings of a Century* (Boston, MA: The Boston History Company, 1896)

Christopher, Anthony J., "Sketches of Yesterday" *The Messenger*, 1960-1973

Clark, Joshua, *Onondaga; or, Reminiscences of earlier and later times; being a series of historical sketches relative to Onondaga; with notes on the several towns in the county, and Oswego* (Syracuse, NY: Stoddard & Babcock, 1849)

Connell, Ruth M. and Christopher, Eleanor T., *Baldwinsville Trolley Trivia* (Written for the Beauchamp Historical Society, 1985)

DeWitt, Benjamin, *Transactions of the Society for the Promotion of Useful Arts 1807*

Feltner, Royal, *Early American Auto Industry, 1869-1929*

Finch, Roy G., *The Story of the New York State Canals, Historical and Commercial Information* (State of New York 1925, Copyright renewed 1998)

Galpin, W. Freeman, *Central New York an Inland Empire*

Gazette and Farmers' Journal Newspaper (Baldwinsville, NY)

Gazette and Farmers' Journal Semi-Centennial Edition

Gordon, William R. and McFarlane, James R., *The Rochester, Syracuse and Eastern "Travelectric" 1906-1931*

Hall, Edith, *The History of Baldwinsville* (Baldwinsville, NY: McHarrie's Legacy, 1981, 1936).

Hand, M.C., *From a Forest to a City, Personal Reminiscences of Syracuse, New York* (Syracuse, NY, 1889)

Hedrick, Ulysses Prentiss, *A History of Agriculture in the State of New York*

History About Syracuse Airport, *Syracuse Hancock International Airport*

History of the Town of Camillus, *Town of Camillus*

Kimes, Beverly Rae, *Pioneers, Engineers and Scoundrels*, (SAE International, 2004)

Klein, Daniel B., Santa Clara University & Majewski, John, University of California-Santa Barbara *Turnpikes and Toll Roads in Nineteenth-Century America*

Langdon, William Chauncy, *Everyday Things in American Life 1776-1876*, (New York, Charles Scribners Sons, 1941)

Larkin, F. Daniel, *New York State Canals - A Short History* (Purple Mountain Press 1998)

McManus, Sue Ellen, *Greater Baldwinsville* (Charleston, SC: Arcadia Publishing Co., 2010)

New York Spectator

New York State Division of Archives and History, *The Sullivan-Clinton Campaign in 1779*

New York State Museum, *The Canal Company*

Nostrant, Robert F., *Steam Canal Boats on the Erie Canal* (Baldwinsville 2002)

Nostrant, Robert F., *The Syracuse and Baldwinsville Railroad* (Baldwinsville 1998)

Onondaga Register

Palmer, Miss L. Pearl, *Historical Review of the Town of Lysander* with additional name and subject indexes compiled by Robert F. Nostrant and Jane H. Kinsley, Margaret C. Bye (Baldwinsville, NY: Town of Lysander, 1997, 1947)

Sadowski, Frank E., Jr., *The Erie Canal - Boats on the Erie Canal* (Dragon Design Associates 2010)

Scisco, Louis Dow, *Early History of the Town of Van Buren, Onondaga County, NY* (Baldwinsville, NY, W.F. Morris Publishing Co., 1895)

Sweet's New Atlas of Onondaga Co. New York: from recent and actual surveys and records under the superintendence of Homer D.L. Sweet (NY: Walker Bros. & Co.,1874)

Syracuse Post-Standard

Syracuse Standard

Town of Lysander, *Book of Highways*

Town of Lysander, *Survey of Roads 1805-1894*

Town of Lysander, *Minute Book of the Lysander Town Board 1836-1893*

Town of Lysander, *Minute Book of the Lysander Town Board 1893-1911, 1911-*

Town of Van Buren, *Minutes of the Van Buren Town Board*

Utica Daily Press

Wise, Andrew W., *The History of Vehicle and Traffic Law*

Whitford, Noble E., *History of the Barge Canal of New York State,* (Supplement to the Annual Report of the State Engineer and Surveyor for the Year Ended June 30, 1921, Albany 1922)

Historical Collections at the Baldwinsville Public Library and The Museum at the Shacksboro Schoolhouse and Town of Lysander Historians Files (Baldwinsville, NY).

Index

www.ingramcontent.com/pod-product-compliance
Lightning Source LLC
Chambersburg PA
CBHW081151090426
42736CB00017B/3275